FORUGH FARROKHZAD

ANOTHER BIRTH
AND OTHER POEMS

Translated by
Hasan Javadi and Susan Sallée

Introduction by
Hasan Javadi

MAGE PUBLISHERS

Library of Congress Cataloging-in-Publication Data

Farrukhzad, Furugh.
[Tavalludi digar. English & Persian]
Another birth and other poems / Forugh Farrokhzad ; translated with an introduction by Hasan Javadi and Susan Sallée. – [Updated and revised ed.].
p. cm.
Includes bibliographical references.
ISBN 1-933823-37-2 (pbk. original : alk. paper)
I. Javadi, Hasan. II. Sallée, Susan. III. Title.
PK6561.F264T3813 2010
891'.5513–dc22

2010004762

978-193382337-9
1-933823-37-2

Mage books are available at bookstores, through the internet, or directly from the publisher:
Mage Publishers, Washington, DC
202-342-1642 • as@mage.com • 800-962-0922
visit Mage Publishers online at
w w w . m a g e . c o m

Contents

Translators' Note

This collection of poems, first published in English in 1981, (together with a companion volume of the Persian text), introduced Forugh Farrokhzad's poetry to an English-speaking audience. Now, in this new, revised and updated edition, we have included the Persian text of the poems on facing pages. We have also added some photos, letters, and a timeline of Forugh's life to give the reader a better understanding of the poet, who remains as relevant today as she was when her daring poems were first published in Iran in the 1960s.

The effort in these translations has been towards as literal a rendition as possible in word, thought, and poetic form. An attempt has also been made to create translations in English that would show some of the poeticality of the originals – that would preserve some qualities of the rhythm and sound which so greatly affect the poems' mood and meaning. Occasional compromises were inevitably necessary to achieve a balance between these two ends, though it is hoped that any departures from the letter of the original will be considered slight, and justified by the effort to find an English idiom that approximates the poetic texture of Forugh's Persian.

Acknowledgement

We would like to express our appreciation to the late Dr. Ardavan Davaran for allowing us to include his article on "The Conquest of the Garden" in this volume. Dr. Davaran, formerly a professor of English Literature at the University of Tehran, and later at Notre Dame de Namur university in California, devoted a significant portion of his doctoral dissertation to modern poetry in general and to the poetry of Forugh Farrokhzad in particular. Ardavan Davaran died in January 2009.

We would also like to thank Farinaz Firouzi for her work on the editing of this revised edition.

INTRODUCTION

Born in Tehran in 1935, Forugh Farrokhzad's early life did not differ greatly from the lives of many other women of the Iranian upper middle class. She attended high school up to the ninth grade, after which she went to the Kamal al-Molk technical school. There, she studied painting and embroidery, both considered to be fashionable arts for young women. At sixteen she fell in love with a neighbor and distant relative, Parviz Shapur. He was a satirist and cartoonist and fifteen years older than her. In spite of parental objection, Forugh married him and they moved to Ahvaz, where he found a job at the Ministry of Finance. Forugh gave birth to her only child, son called Kamyar, a year later. After three years, Forugh decided to leave her husband. In those days

ABOVE: Family photo showing Forugh and her older brother Amir, in uniform, seated either side of their mother, together with her older sister and younger brother. Her father towers over the family in his lieutenant's uniform. FACING PAGE: Above, Forugh at age 12, and below, with her son, Kamyar, and husband Parviz Shapur.

Forugh with her son Kamyar

a woman asking for a divorce was taboo in Iran, and the full guardianship of the child almost always went to the father. Forugh was denied even occasional visitation rights to Kamyar, which left an indelible mark on her life and poetry. Perhaps it was because of this that she suffered a nervous breakdown in September 1955 and was admitted to a psychiatric clinic in Tehran.

After recovering, Forugh who had published her first collection of poetry *Asir* (The Captive) in 1955, published a second collection *Divar* (The Wall). Soon after, she developed an interest in cinematography, acting and producing. The sensation created as a reaction to her willingness to express her honest and sensual feminine feelings in the male-dominated literary and artistic society of Iran combined with her free lifestyle caused such a stir that she felt she had to get away before the publication of her third collection *Osian* (Rebellion, 1957). She went to Italy in 1956 to study cinematography and art (and perhaps to escape slandering tongues). Her trip to Italy lasted nine months, after which she visited her older brother who was studying medicine in Munich. There, she also learned some German and with the help of her brother translated an anthology of twenty-nine German poets of the first half of the twentieth century. It was published posthumously in 1980 as *Marg-e man ruzi fara khahad resid* (My Death Will Come One Day). The title is borrowed from a poem by the German poet Ossip Kalenter (1900-1976), which inspired her to also write her own epitaph entitled "B`adha" (Afterwards).

Returning to Iran, Forugh became the assistant to Ebrahim Golestan, a talented filmmaker and literary figure. Though married and thirteen years her senior, Forugh fell in love with him and they lived together – another scandal in Iranian literary circles. In 1960, depressed by family and financial problems and separation from her son, she unsuccessfully attempted suicide by taking sleeping pills.

With the help of Ebrahim Golestan, Forugh made several documentary films, the most outstanding being "The House is Black," based on the lives of lepers in a colony in Tabriz (Baba Baghi). During the production of the film, she lived for twelve days in this colony and associated freely with the lepers. Forugh adopted a leper, Hasan Mansuri, from his parents. The film won the prize for best documentary film in the Oberhausen Film Festival in Germany in 1963.

Ebrahim Golestan not only guided Forugh through the world of cinema, he also helped her in reading and translating poets like T. S. Eliot, Ezra Pound and Edith Sitwell. Bahman Sholevar, a talented novelist and translator, and apparently also her lover for a period, helped her as well to become familiar with English poets. At the same time Forugh's familiarity with Persian poetry was becoming more extensive. She says of her earlier days before she produced her three early collections: "Because I was reading collection after collection of poetry, I was saturated, and since I was saturated, and I had at any rate a bit of talent too, I inevitably had to pour it back somehow. I don't know if these were poems or not. I only know that there were many 'I's' in those days, and they were all sincere. And I know that they were also very easy. I was not formed yet. I had not found my own language, my own form and intellectual world. I was in the small and narrow environment we call 'family life.' Then suddenly I was emptied of all those things. I changed my surroundings; that is, they changed naturally and by themselves."

ABOVE: Forugh with camera, directing her film "The House is Black." FACING PAGE: Forugh acting in the Luigi Pirandello play, *Six Characters in Search of an Author.*

Forugh published four collections of poetry during her lifetime: *Asir* (*The Captive*, 1955), at the age of seventeen; *Divar* (*The Wall*, 1956); *Osian* (*Rebellion*, 1957); and *Tavalodi Digar* (*Another Birth*, 1963). Her fifth collection, *Iman Biyavarim be Aghaz-e Fasl-e Sard (Let Us Believe in the Beginning of the Cold Season)*, was posthumously published in 1974. These five volumes fall into two distinct categories. The three early collections consist almost entirely of introspective and confessional poems in a traditional lyric style. As the titles suggest, the poet is exploring her identity as a woman entrapped in a society of traditional mores and values. Love – sexual and romantic – is the primary theme throughout the first two collections, serving for Forugh as a means of self-expression and social protest. In the third volume. The questioning of conventional religious beliefs becomes the dominant theme. In *Another Birth* and *Let Us Believe in the Beginning of the Cold Season*, Forugh broadens her vision of the world. She experiences a "rebirth" and becomes concerned not only with her personal conflicts but with the predicaments of society as a whole.

It was in the last decade of her life, or more exactly with the publication of *Tavalodi Digar (Another Birth)* in 1963, that Forugh found her proper medium and language, and in this the influence of Nima,* the founder of modern Persian poetry, was unmistakable. Forugh says that Nima was like Hafez† for her.

* Nima Yushij *(1895-1960)* was the founder of modern Persian poetry
† Hafez (d. 1326) is considered the greatest lyric poet of Iran.

"He was my guide, but I was my own maker. I always relied upon my own experiences. I had to discover first of all how it was that Nima arrived at that language and form. If I hadn't discovered (that myself), it would have had no use, I would have been an unscrupulous imitator. I had to traverse that road – that is, I had to live. When I say 'I had to,' this 'had to' explains and interprets a sort of natural and instinctive hard-headedness in me. Besides Nima, many [poets] have enchanted me, like Shamlu. From the point of view of my sentiments and poetic taste, he is the closest poet [to me]"

Forugh herself did not think highly of her three early volumes, claiming that her poetry really began with *Another Birth*. The early collections are imitative of both contemporary and classical Persian poetry, as well as of some Western verse, and it is only with the last two collections that Forugh truly establishes herself as an impressive and talented poet. The influence of certain Western poets remains in some poems of the later collections. Passages from the poem "Another Birth," or from the long poem "Let Us Believe in the Beginning of the Cold Season," for instance, remind one of T. S. Eliot's *Wasteland*, and the tone of "Earthly Verses" echoes that of the *Bible* and *Paradise Lost*. Trace of certain Iranian poets can also still be detected. Among them, Hafez and Nima Yushij seem to have had the greatest impact, a fact that Forugh herself acknowledged in some of her interviews. But these influences are absorbed and reproduced in Forugh's later work in a voice – both fresh and original – of her own. It is therefore the later volumes that bear the hallmark of Forugh at her best.

The early collections, however, are important in tracing the development of Forugh's personality and poetic gift. In this early phase, Forugh typifies the intellectual Iranian woman caught in the cross-tides of a strict, traditional society and the ever-increasing onslaught of Western ideas and modes of life. In *The Captive* Forugh finds herself facing the harsh realities of an Iranian woman whose romantic ideas of love and marriage are shattered overnight. Her poems often explicitly reflect the problems confronting her in her actual life, imprisoned in a loveless marriage. In the poem "*The Captive*," for instance, she likens herself to a caged bird, hoping to be set free by her lover, yet aware that the price of such freedom will be to leave her son behind:

> *If, O sky, I want one day to fly*
> *Out from this silent prison, cold and stern,*

What shall I say to the child's weeping eyes?
Forget about me, for I'm a captive bird.

The bondage of woman in marriage is exemplified in another poem, not translated in the present volume, entitled "The Wedding Ring." At first the gold ring signifies happiness and life to the young bride, but as the years pass she comes to see it as a ring of enslavement to a man who does not honor the spiritual bonds of marriage. In "Runaway" *(Ramideh)* Forugh expresses, in perhaps a more general way, the agony of living amidst a world that cannot understand, much less condone, the desires that arise and stir in her inner life. There, she also asserts the independence that ultimately characterizes Forugh as a personality and as a poet – that despite the pain of alienation, it is ultimately to herself and her verse that she will be true:

My heart, O mad, mad heart of mine,
That from this alienation still does burn,
Make no more your plaint at strangers' hands,
For God's sake, cease, and from this madness turn.

The Wall, which opens with a *ghazal* by Hafez and with quotations from Khayyam, Milton, and Goethe, continues the lyrical poetic form and attempts to imitate the purity of Hafez's lyricism. Forugh is still hoping that her lover will fulfill her romantic ideals and transport her from "this city of sorrows."* In *The Wall*, as in *The Captive*, Forugh openly and boldly expresses her innermost feelings of love and sexuality. This freedom of expression is something we may take for granted today, but for an Iranian woman of Forugh's time it was extremely shocking and daring. No poet of Iran before her had spoken so candidly, and such explicitness was considered highly immoral. Somewhat like D. H. Lawrence, Forugh celebrates love and sex because they are integral and natural to human life. She extols sensuality and love as if to console herself through their expression and to lash out at the hypocrisies of a repressive world. This defiance is evident in a poem like "Sin," where she somewhat proudly confesses:

I have sinned, a delectable sin,
In an embrace which was ardent like fire.

---

* "Roya," *Divar* (Tehran *1973), p. 23.*

I have sinned in the midst of arms
Which were hot and vengeful, like iron.

In both *The Wall* and *The Captive*, however, a sense of guilt is occasionally present amidst the defiant self-assertion – a vestige of the restraints of her upbringing and social background. In the last stanza of "Sin," it is almost an apology that falters on her lips:

I have sinned, a delectable sin,
Beside a body, trembling and dazed.
God, how can I know what I did
In that dark and silent, private place?

And even in the poem "Bathing," which celebrates a pure form of sensuality in a sylvan setting and not an overtly sexual scene, the weight of social conditioning is nonetheless felt as her body revels in "the spirit of that sinful spring."

As Forugh's rebelliousness and self-assertion grow bolder the sense of guilt is forgotten. In her third volume, *Rebellion*, in the tri-part title poem, Forugh questions the entire system of creation as outlined in the *Qur'an* or the *Bible*. She challenges, for instance, the notion that God was justified when He created Satan:

It was you, it was you who from a flame
Such a demon made and set on the road.

The poem resembles some of the most daring quatrains of Khayyam or the famous poem attributed to Naser Khosrow on the subject of man and sin. Forugh, like Khayyam, would prefer a world where "the lover attains her beloved easily,"* and her rebellion stems from the fact that neither her birth nor her destiny are in her hands. "I came into the world without being 'I'," she complains; "I saw myself in the mirror, void of self." She questions a God who brings his creatures into the world and dominates their fates. He makes them lovers of beauty and infuses them with love, and then blames them for their actions. The entire system is, in short, unfair.

* Omar Khayyam, quoted by Forugh in *Osian* (Tehran *1972), p. 39.*

Though many of the poems in *Rebellion* are similar in their lyrical nature to those of Forugh's first two volumes, social concerns, and more particularly the plight of women, become more dominant themes. The personal and the social are often interwoven. In poems like "Return" and "A Poem for You," Forugh expresses her frustration with a society which out of prudish hypocrisy does not allow her to see her son. In "A Poem for You" she affirms her wish "to be the voice of my own existence," but complains of the impossibility of fulfilling such a wish: "But alas, a 'woman' was I." Turning to her son she says:

When over this confused book with no beginning
Your innocent eyes are drawn,
You will see the rooted rebellion of years
Has bloomed in the heart of every song

In *Another Birth* Forugh further develops her thoughts about the plight of women. Her spirit of personal rebellion, however, gives way to a socially wider expression of intolerance towards women who, for the sake of security and comfort, "defile the chastity of love" in the bed of "a drunk, a vagrant, a fool." Like Nora in Ibsen's *A Doll's House*, Forugh vehemently defends the dignity of womanhood, and she bitterly rebukes those who resign themselves to their fate:

You can be just like a mechanical doll
and view your world with two glass eyes
You can sleep in a cloth-lined box for years
with a body stuffed with straw
in the folds of lace and sequins.
You can cry out and say for no reason at all
with every lascivious squeeze of a hand:
"Ah, how lucky I am!"

Thus the personal scope of experience expressed in Forugh's first three volumes has led to a larger vision and sentiment towards women's position in modern times.

The publication of *Another Birth* in 1963 does indeed mark a new phase in Forugh's work. By the consensus of the critics and according to Forugh herself, *Another Birth* and the last posthumous volume contain the poetry of Forugh at her best. The poems gain a new dimension and perspective, and begin to question the fate of modern man in general. Social concern is not totally absent in the earlier collections, either, but, as we have seen, the tone in those works is dominantly personal. With *Another Birth* and *Let Us Believe in the Beginning of the Cold Season,* the center of gravity shifts. The search for personal identity is now largely absorbed in the search for identity and purpose in society as a whole, and the visionary voice of poetry becomes finally the very means through which Forugh ascertains her own much-sought-for identity. Several poems in *Another Birth* can be seen as direct social commentaries. Confusion and lack of direction in the world Forugh observes around her are the primary themes, for instance, of the long satirical poem "O Bejewelled Land." The title refers to the name of a patriotic song, and the whole poem is a scathing criticism of Iranian bureaucracy [where a person's identity can only be proven by the omnipotent ID card]. The theme of social banality and decadence continues in *Let Us Believe in the Beginning of the Cold Season* in poems such as "My Heart Grieves for the Garden," for example. Here, Forugh portrays her own sister living in the upper-class part of town in her artificial house, and with her artificial husband, her artificial apple trees, and her artificial songs – an unending falseness except for the "natural babies" she continually bears into this artificial and plastic world. Forugh carries the bite of her criticism to each family member in turn, each representing a particular social segment with their attitudes and futile modes of life that blind them to the decadence and danger that surrounds them.

It is perhaps because of the decay that Forugh perceives pervading her society and her world that loneliness becomes a dominant theme and mood in her later poetry. This loneliness often evokes in Forugh memories of childhood, with their sharply contrasting sensibility of life, excitement and warmth. In the poems "In the Cold Streets of Night" and "The Loneliness of the Moon" (the latter not translated in the present volume), no sound remains but the "goodbye, goodbye" of parting couples. In the title poem of *Let Us Believe in the Beginning of the Cold Season* we find Forugh at age thirty-two "a lonely woman on the threshold of a cold season." On the streets the wind is blowing, and "lonely retrieving crows/circle in the old gardens of inertia." The poem "Friday" also exemplifies this pervasive sense of loneliness; all of Forugh's feelings of depression, solitude and languor are distilled into the space of three stanzas, and yet they are merged with a sense of nostalgic recollection that once there existed a fuller and more vital time:

Ah, how proudly and quietly it passed!
My life, like a strange stream
in the heart of these silent, deserted Fridays
in the heart of these houses, depressing and empty,
Ah, how proudly and quietly it passed...

Images of night and mechanization, of "clamoring crowds" and rotting vegetation,* infiltrate Forugh's poetic world. In the tersely powerful poem "My Heart Grieves," we find that "The lamp of connection is dark." Even human love is seen to be stifling within this estranged and spiritually death-like scene, as in the poem, "Couple," where after lovemaking there is no real union between the lovers and "two hearts" ultimately equate "two solitudes."

Death begins to emerge as an image and theme in these later poems of Forugh. The vision of "Earthly Verses" perhaps conveys most strikingly this mounting sense of gloom, anxiety and preoccupation with death. The sun has grown cold; fish and grass, life and verdure, have dried. Birth brings only "headless babes," and even its regenerative potential is gone, for "the earth no longer took unto itself/the dead." It is a land where cruelty and perversion prevail, where men cut each other's throats with knives and "sleep with prepubescent girls/in beds of blood." It is small wonder that rites of execution excite "their old and tired nerves," as if terror and death have in fact become a substitute for the life and love that no one thinks of anymore in these "dark and bitter" days.

Alongside such terrifying poems, though, there are in Forugh's later volumes some lyrical pieces of superb beauty. The lyricism sometimes consists of a highly sensitive depiction of childhood memories arising as a release and antidote to the present sense of frustration and decay. There are also love songs, however, where Forugh reaches a level of poetic beauty and lyricism that is not just in reaction to the dismay she feels at her world. Rather, they seem to belong to the emergence of a new vision, or to the expression of a side of Forugh's inner world that, despite the surrounding decadence, has not died. "The Sun Rises," for instance, with an almost ecstatic rhythm that cannot be adequately reproduced in translation, is not unlike some of the most

* As for instance, in "Those Days," *p. 37* of the present volume.

superb mystical ghazals of Jalaluddin Rumi's *Divan-e Shams.** In the poem we see Forugh's lover coming to take her far away, to the "city where verses and passions bloom," to the "lands of light and of perfume" from whence he came. Less ecstatic, but nonetheless with a similar outlook of love and faith, is "The Wind Will Take Us Away," or "I Will Greet the Sun Once Again," where Forugh affirms that she will "greet once again/those who love, and the girl/still standing on the threshold filled with love."

Thus, while Forugh's vision in her later work is predominantly one of darkness, there are glimmers of hope, intimations of brightness. The theme of rebirth, of death and new growth, comes to figure centrally in her verse, creating a bridge between the diverse sentiments of bitter gloom and lyric affirmation. In "Another Birth," despite the corruption and decay there are many references to regeneration and growth.

Forugh consistently conceives of rebirth in the imagery of nature's abundance and regeneration. In "I Will Greet the Sun Once Again" Forugh herself becomes part of nature, sensing and internalizing its outward forms as affirmative aspects of her own being. She greets the streams that flowed within her, the clouds that were her tallest thoughts and the earth whose burning womb she filled with green seeds in her "lust for repetition." In "It Is Only the Voice that Remains," she acknowledges the inevitability of death, but sees it as part of a larger natural whole. Thus she connects herself again with nature to intimate regeneration: "I place the unripe ears of wheat/beneath my breast/ and give them milk." Nature is life and birth and love, and in its processes are contained the hope of salvation from decay and death. Her connection with nature leads her at times to a large and even prophetic vision, as in "Walls of Frontier" where she concludes:

Let me be impregnated by the moon
Let me be filled
with the little drops of rain
with the heart yet to be formed
with the children yet to be born
that perhaps my love
will become the cradle for another Christ.

* Rumi *(1207-1273)* was one of the greatest classical poets and mystics of Iran.

In tracing the development of Forugh's poetry as a whole, then, we witness a movement from the introspective and rather limited treatment of love and sexuality in her early work to a broader view where self-exploration is conducted through the simultaneous examination of the surrounding world. The movement is clearly not *away* from the self, but rather toward an understanding of self through the perception and confrontation of larger realities – both the gloomy social realities of a modern, mechanized world, and the faith-inspiring realities of the natural, regenerative one. The development of Forugh's poetry thus reflects her own inward search, which she expressed in a letter to he lover, Ebrahim Golestan: "I want to pierce everything and as much as possible to penetrate into all things. I want to reach the depths of the earth. My love is there – the place where the seeds grow and the roots reach each other, and creation continues amidst decay. It is as if my body is a transient form of this action."* And if her body is a transient form of nature's creative action, then her poetry certainly lives on to express it; for with the wider vision of her mature work, Forugh attained a level of art that transcends the limits of a single time or place. It is perhaps prophetic of her own verse that Forugh writes in one of her final poems, 'It Is Only the Voice that Remains":

The voice, the voice, only the voice
the voice of the translucent desire of water to flow
the voice of starlight pouring on the surface of the pistil of the earth
the voice of the conception of the seed of meaning
and the expansion of love's common mind
The voice, the voice, the voice, it is only the voice that remains.

A yearning for freedom, a sense of defiance of repression, and hope for a revolution have always existed in modern Persian poetry: "The Winter" by Mehdi Akhavan-Saless, depicted the harsh, repressive atmosphere of the Shah's era; in the "Dead-end," Ahmad Shamlu wrote, "they smell your breath, lest you've said 'I love you.' They search your thoughts. And one must hide God in the closet." Similarly, in the poetry of Forugh a sense of rebellious yearning for a breathing space is apparent. Forugh fought two battles: while she revolted against repression in an undemocratic society, she was also fighting for the rights of women who were doubly repressed. She was not only a unique and talented poet, but she also distinguished herself as a woman who

* Translated from Amir Isma'ili, *Javedaneh Forugh Farrokhzad* (Tehran 1968), p. 14.

dared to express her innermost feelings about love, sex, society and the self with an openness and frankness unprecedented in Persian literature. She can be considered as one of the forerunners of the Iranian Women's Movement of recent years, whose daring and heroic examples we have witnessed as part of the Green Movement. Perhaps it is prophetic that Forugh, in spite of the despair in much of her poetry, believes, in regeneration and rebirth. She says, in her poem "Another Birth":

I plant my hands in the garden
I will grow green, I know, I know, I know
and in the hollows of my ink-stained fingers
swallows will lay eggs

At last, Forugh has found a poetic connection of cosmic scale both with nature and with her people.

* * *

Forugh died at 32, from head injuries in a car accident, at the height of her creative powers. She swerved the jeep she was driving to avoid an oncoming vehicle. The jeep hit a wall and she was thrown out hitting her head on the curb. She was buried, while snow fell, at the Zahir-al Dowleh cemetery in the foothills of Tehran.

A page of one of Forugh's poems in her own handwriting.

فرخ زاد

پنجره . ص ۲

و سارهای سراسیمه از درخت کهنسال پر زدند

من از میان ریشه‌های گیاهان گوشتخوار می‌آیم

و مغز من هنوز

لبریز از صدای وحشت پروانه‌ایست که او را

در دفتری به سنجاقی

مصلوب کرده بودند

× × ×

وقتی که اعتماد من از ریسمان سست عدالت آویزان بود

در تمام شهر

قلب چراغ‌های مرا تکه تکه می‌کردند

وقتی که چشم‌های کودکانهٔ عشق مرا

با دستمال تیرهٔ قانون می‌بستند

و از شقیقه‌های مضطرب آرزوی من

فواره‌های خون به بیرون می‌پاشید

وقتی که زندگی من دیگر

چیزی نبود، هیچ چیز بجز تیک تاک ساعت دیواری

دریافتم که باید

باید

باید

... دیوانه‌وار دوست بدارم

× × ×

اسیر

ترا میخواهم و دانم که هرگز
به کام دل در آغوشت نگیرم
توئی آن آسمان صاف و روشن
من این کنج قفس، مرغی اسیرم

ز پشت میله های سرد و تیره
نگاه حسرتم حیران به رویت
در این فکرم که دستی پیش آید
و من ناگه گشایم پر بسویت

در این فکرم که در یك لحظه غفلت
از این زندان خامش پر بگیرم
به چشم مرد زندانبان بخندم
کنارت زندگی از سر بگیرم

در این فکرم من و دانم که هرگز
مرا یارای رفتن زین قفس نیست
اگر هم مرد زندانبان بخواهد
دگر از بهر پروازم نفس نیست

ز پشت میله ها، هر صبح روشن
نگاه کودکی خندد برویم
چو من سر میکنم آواز شادی
لبش با بوسه می آید بسویم

اگر ای آسمان خواهم که یکروز
از این زندان خامش پر بگیرم
به چشم کودك گریان چه گویم
زمن بگذر، که من مرغی اسیرم

The Captive

I want you, yet I know I'll never
Attain my heart's desire in your embrace;
You are that pure and luminous sky,
I, a captive bird in this corner of the cage.

From behind the cold, dark bars,
My sorrow's bewildered look upon your face,
I'm thinking there might come a hand
And toward you I will spread my wings apace.

I am thinking that in a moment of neglect,
Out from this silent prison I will fly,
Laugh in the face of the man who jails me,
And then begin life over by your side.

I am thinking this, and know that never
Will I have the strength to leave from out this cage;
Even if the man who jails should wish it,
Breath for my flight no longer now remains.

Each bright morning, from behind the bars,
Before me a child's look laughs with bliss;
When I start singing a song of joy,
His lips take wing toward me with a kiss.

If, O sky, I want one day to fly
Out from his silent prison, cold and stern,
What shall I say to the child's weeping eyes?
Forget about me, for I'm a captive bird.

من آن شمعم که با سوز دل خویش
فروزان میکنم ویرانه‌ای را
اگر خواهم که خاموشی گزینم
پریشان میکنم کاشانه‌ای را

I am that candle, who with my burning heart
Make a ruin glow;
If I choose to snuff out the light,
I will destroy a nest.

رمیده

نمیدانم چه میخواهم خدایا
بدنبال چه میگردم شب و روز
چه میجوید نگاه خسته من
چرا افسرده است این قلب پر سوز

ز جمع آشنایان میگریزم
به کنجی میخزم آرام و خاموش
نگاهم غوطه ور در تیرگیها
به بیمار دل خود میدهم گوش

گریزانم از این مردم که با من
بظاهر همدم و یکرنگ هستند
ولی در باطن از فرط حقارت
بدامانم دو صد پیرایه بستند

از این مردم، که تا شعرم شنیدند
برویم چون گلی خوشبو شکفتند
ولی آندم که در خلوت نشستند
مرا دیوانه‌ای بد نام گفتند

دل من، ای دل دیوانه من
که میسوزی از این بیگانگی ها
مکن دیگر ز دست غیر فریاد
خدا را، بس کن این دیوانگی ها

Runaway[*]

I do not know, O God, what I desire,
What it is I seek both night and day,
What my tired eyes are looking for,
Why this burning heart is so dismayed.

From gatherings of friends I run away,
And to a corner, quiet and calm, I creep,
Listening to the ailments of my heart,
My vision plunged in shadows dark and deep.

I flee from all these people who with me
To friendship and sincerity pretend,
But inwardly, replete with paltriness,
Tie two hundred spangles to my hem.[†]

These people, when they hear my poetry,
Smile like fragrant flowers to my face,
But call me a mad woman of ill fame
When sitting in their own secluded place.

My heart, O mad, mad heart of mine,
That from this alienation still does burn,
Make no more your plaint at strangers' hands,
For God's sake, cease, and from this madness turn.

---

* Runaway, *Ramideh* in Persian connotes an animal running away when startled. In poetry, the word has been used to refer to a beloved who has left the lover.

† In Persian, the image of "tying spangles to my hem" connotes "staining my reputation."

گناه

گنه کردم گناهی پر ز لذت
در آغوشی که گرم و آتشین بود
گنه کردم میان بازوانی
که داغ و کینه جوی و آهنین بود

در آن خلوتگه تاریك و خاموش
نگه کردم بچشم پر ز رازش
دلم در سینه بی تابانه لرزید
ز خواهش های چشم پر نیازش

در آن خلوتگه تاریك و خاموش
پریشان در کنار او نشستم
لبش بر روی لبهایم هوس ریخت
ز اندوه دل دیوانه رستم

فرو خواندم بگوشش قصه عشق:
ترا میخواهم ای جانانه من
ترا میخواهم ای آغوش جانبخش
ترا، ای عاشق دیوانه من

هوس در دیدگانش شعله افروخت
شراب سرخ در پیمانه رقصید
تن من در میان بستر نرم
بروی سینه اش مستانه لرزید

گنه کردم گناهی پر زلذت
کنار پیکری لرزان و مدهوش
خداوندا چه میدانم چه کردم
در آن خلوتگه تاریك و خاموش

Sin

I have sinned, a delectable sin
In an embrace which was ardent, like fire
I have sinned in the midst of arms
Which were hot and vengeful, like iron

In that dark and silent private place
I looked to his secret-filled eyes
In my breast my heart trembled anxiously
In desire of his entreating eyes

In that dark and silent private place
I sat, distracted, by his side
His lips poured passion upon mine
I was saved from my mad heart's sorrows

I whispered the tale of love in his ear:
I want you, O sweetheart of mine
I want you, O life-giving bosom, You,
O mad love of mine

Passion kindled flames in his eyes
The red wine danced in the glass
In the soft bed, against his chest
My body trembled with drunkenness

I have sinned, a delectable sin
Beside a body, trembling and dazed
O God, how can I know what I did
In that dark and silent private place?

آبتنی

لخت شدم تا در آن هوای دل انگیز
پیکر خود را به آب چشمه بشویم
وسوسه میریخت بر دلم شب خاموش
تا غم دل را بگوش چشمه بگویم

آب خنك بود و موجهای درخشان
ناله کنان گرد من به شوق خزیدند
گوئی با دستهای نرم و بلورین
جان و تنم را بسوی خویش کشیدند

بادی از آن دورها وزید و شتابان
دامنی از گل بروی گیسوی من ریخت
عطر دلاویز و تند پونه وحشی
از نفس باد در مشام من آویخت

چشم فرو بستم و خموش و سبکروح
تن به علف های نرم و تازه فشردم
همچون زنی کاو غنوده در بر معشوق
یکسره خود را به دست چشمه سپردم

روی دو ساقم لبان مرتعش آب
بوسه زن و بیقرار و تشنه و تبدار
ناگه در هم خزید ... راضی و سرمست
جسم من و روح چشمه سار گنه کار

Bathing

Naked I stood in that heart-stirring air
To bathe in the waters of the spring;
Night's hush poured temptation on my heart
To tell its sorrow to the ear of the spring.

The water was cool, and sparkling waves
Crept 'round me, moaning with passion
As if they drew me, body and soul
With soft, crystal hands in their direction.

There blew from afar a breeze that poured
An apron of flowers hastily upon my hair;
The sharp, fragrant scent of wild pennyroyal clung
To my nostrils from the breath of the wafting air.

I closed my eyes, silent, free of care
Pressed my body to the soft new grass;
Like a woman reclining in her lover's arms
Into the hands of the spring I let myself pass.

Then at once on my legs its trembling lips
Crept kissing, fevered, thirsting and restless.
Drunken and thoroughly pleased, my body
Mixed with the spirit of that sinful spring.

گمشده

بعد از آن دیوانگی ها ای دریغ
باورم ناید که عاقل گشته‌ام
گوئیا «او» مرده در من کین چنین
خسته و خاموش و باطل گشته‌ام

هردم از آئینه میپرسم ملول
چیستم دیگر، بچشمت چیستم ؟
لیك در آئینه میبینم که، وای
سایه‌ای هم زانچه بودم نیستم

همچو آن رقاصه هندو بناز
پای میکوبم ولی بر گور خویش
وه که با صد حسرت این ویرانه را
روشنی بخشیده‌ام از نور خویش

ره نمی جویم بسوی شهر روز
بیگمان در قعر گوری خفته‌ام
گوهری دارم ولی آن را زبیم
در دل مردابها بنهفته‌ام

میروم ... اما نمی پرسم ز خویش
ره کجا ...؟ منزل کجا ...؟ مقصود چیست؟
بوسه می بخشم ولی خود غافلم
کاین دل دیوانه را معبود کیست

«او» چو در من مرد، ناگه هرچه بود
در نگاهم حالتی دیگر گرفت
گوئیا شب با دو دست سرد خویش
روح بی تاب مرا در بر گرفت

Lost

After those acts of madness, ah, alas
I can't believe that I've grown wise
It seems that she has died in me,
I'm so weary, so silent, so nullified

Every moment I ask the mirror in despair,
What am I, at least in your eyes?
But in the mirror I see that I am
Alas, not even a shadow of what I was

Like the Indian dancer, coquettishly
I dance, but upon my own grave
Alas, that with a hundred regrets
I've illumined this ruin with my own rays

I seek not the road to the city of day
Undoubtedly, I sleep in the depths of a grave
A pearl I possess, but out of fear
In the heart of the marshes I hid it away

I walk...but I do not ask of myself
Where's the road, the station, the destination, where?
I give kisses, but am in myself unaware
To whom this mad heart its reverence bears

When she died in me, suddenly, whatever was
In my keeping took on a new tone
It seems that night with its two cold hands
Has drawn to its side my restless soul

آه ... آری ... این منم ... اما چه سود
«او» که در من بود، دیگر، نیست، نیست
میخروشم زیر لب دیوانه وار
«او» که در من بود، آخر کیست، کیست؟

Ah…yes…this is me, but to what avail?
She who was in me is no more, no more
Madly I shout beneath my breath
She who was in me, who was it, after all?

شعری برای تو

این شعر را برای تو میگویم
در یك غروب تشنه تابستان
در نیمه های این ره شوم آغاز
در کهنه گور این غم بی پایان

این آخرین ترانه لالائیست
درپای گاهواره خواب تو
باشد که بانگ وحشی این فریاد
پیچد در آسمان شباب تو

بگذار سایه من سر گردان
از سایه تو، دور وجدا باشد
روزی بهم رسیم که گر باشد
کس بین ما، نه غیر خدا باشد

من تکیه دادهام به دری تاریك
پیشانی فشرده ز دردم را
میسایم از امید بر این در باز
انگشتهای نازك و سردم را

آن داغ ننگ خورده که میخندید
بر طعنه های بیهده، من بودم
گفتم، که بانگ هستی خود باشم
اما دریغ و درد که «زن» بودم

چشمان بیگناه تو چون لغزد
بر این کتاب در هم بی آغاز
عصیان ریشه دار زمانها را
بینی شکفته دردل هر آواز

A Poem for You

I write this poem for you
On a thirsty summer's eve,
Halfway on this ill-starred road,
In the old grave of this endless grief

This is the final lullaby
At the foot of your cradle of sleep
The wild hue of this cry perhaps
Through the sky of your youth will sweep

Let the shadow of me, the wanderer,
Be separate and far from yours
If one day we are joined again
No one but God shall stand between us

Against a darkened door I've leaned
My brow with pain compressed;
Over this open door I run
My cold, thin fingers in hopefulness

I was the one branded with shame
Who laughed at vain taunts and cried:
"Let me be the voice of my own existence!"
But alas, a "woman" was I

When over this confused book with no beginning
Your innocent eyes are drawn,
You will see the rooted rebellion of years
Has bloomed in the heart of every song

اینجا، ستاره‌ها همه خاموشند
اینجا، فرشته‌ها، همه گریانند
اینجا شکوفه‌های گل مریم،
بیقدرتر ز خار بیابانند

اینجا نشسته بر سر هر راهی
دیو دروغ و ننگ و ریاکاری
در آسمان تیره نمیبینم
نوری ز صبح روشن بیداری

بگذار تا دو باره شود لبریز
چشمان من، ز دانه شبنمها
رفتم ز خود که پرده بر اندازم
از چهر پاك حضرت مریم ها

بگسسته‌ام ز ساحل خوشنامی
در سینه‌ام ستاره توفانست
پرواز گاه شعله خشم من
دردا، فضای تیره زندانست

من تکیه داده‌ام به دری تاریك
پیشانی فشرده زدردم را
میسایم از امید بر این در باز
انگشتهای نازك و سردم را

با این گروه زاهد ظاهر ساز
دانم که این جدال نه آسانست
شهر من و تو، طفلك شیرینم
دیریست کاشیانه شیطانست

روزی رسد که چشم تو با حسرت
لغزد بر این ترانه درد آلود
جوئی مرا درون سخنهایم
گوئی بخود که مادر من او بود

Here, the stars are extinguished
Here, weep all the angels
Here, the blossoms of tuberoses
Are less pricey than desert brambles

Here at every road's end there sits
The demon of shame and hypocrisy
The aurora of morning's awakening
In the darksome sky I do not see

Once more, let my eyes be filled
And brimming with drops of dew;
I've parted from myself to lift the veils
From the faces of innocent Madonnas

I am torn from the shore of good repute
There shines in my breast the tempest's star
The range of flight for my anger's flame
Is alas, the space of this prison dark

Against a darkened door I've leaned
My brow with pain compressed;
Over this open door I run
My cold, thin fingers in hopefulness

This ascetic and sanctimonious group
Is not easy, I know, to contest;
Your city and mine, my dear sweet child,
Has long been the devil's nest

The day will come when ruefully
Your eyes over this pained song will play;
In my words you'll search for me
And inwardly "She was my mother" say

بازگشت

عاقبت خط جاده پایان یافت
من رسیدم ز ره غبار آلود
نگهم پیشتر ز من میتاخت
بر لبانم سلام گرمی بود

شهر جوشان درون کوزه ظهر
کوچه می سوخت در تب خورشید
پای من روی سنگفرش خموش
پیش می رفت و سخت میلرزید

خانه ها رنگ دیگری بودند
گرد آلوده، تیره و دلگیر
چهره‌ها در میان چادرها
همچو ارواح پای در زنجیر

جوی خشکیده، همچو چشمی کور
خالی از آب و از نشانه او
مردی آوازه خوان ز راه گذشت
گوش من پر شد از ترانه او

گنبد آشنای مسجد پیر
کاسه‌های شکسته را میماند
مؤمنی بر فراز گلدسته
با نوائی حزین اذان میخواند

میدویدند از پی سگها
کودکان پا برهنه، سنگ به دست
زنی از پشت معجری خندید
باد نا گه دریچه‌ای را بست

Return

The ribbon of road ended at last,
Covered with dust I arrived;
My glance rushed on ahead of me,
On my lips a warm greeting smiled

The city boiled in the cauldron of noon,
The street burned in the fever of sun;
My feet on the silent stone pavement
Trembled hard and forward did run

The houses had donned a different hue
Dusty, depressing, in darkness steeped;
The faces that peered from between the veils
Were like ghosts with chained and fettered feet

The dried-up stream, like a blind eye,
Was of water void, of his vestige free;
A man passed by, singing a song,
My ears were filled with his melody

The familiar dome of the old mosque
Looked like a cracked and broken bowl;
A believer atop the minaret sang
The call to prayer with a song of dole

The children were running after the dogs,
Barefoot, with stones in hand;
A woman laughed from behind a fence,
In the wind a window suddenly slammed

از دهان سیاه هشتی ها
بوی نمناك گور میآمد
مرد کوری عصا زنان میرفت
آشنائی ز دور میآمد

دری آنجا گشوده گشت خموش
دستهائی مرا بخود خواندند
اشکی از ابر چشمها بارید
دستهائی مرا ز خود راندند

روی دیوار باز پیچك پیر
موج میزد چو چشمه‌ای لرزان
بر تن برگهای انبوهش
سبزی پیری و غبار زمان

نگهم جستجو کنان پرسید
«در کدامین مکان نشانه اوست؟»
لیك دیدم اتاق کوچك من
خالی از بانگ کودکانه اوست

از دل خاك سرد آئینه
ناگهان پیکرش چو گل روئید
موج زد دیدگان مخملیش
آه، در وهم هم مرا میدید!

تکیه دادم به سینه دیوار
گفتم آهسته: «این توئی کامی؟»
لیك دیدم کز آن گذشته تلخ
هیچ باقی نمانده جز نامی

From out the dark mouth of vestibules
Came the damp, dank smell of the grave;
A blind man walked tapping his cane,
From afar a familiar face wended its way

A door silently, quietly, opened there,
Some hands called me to themselves;
From the cloud of the eyes a tear rained down,
Some hands drove me from themselves

Like a trembling spring, on the wall once more
There rippled the old ivy vine;
On the body of its dense foliage
Sat the green of old age and the dust of time

Searchingly my glance inquired:
"Where is there a sign of him, O where?"
But I saw my tiny little room
Was devoid of his childish cries

From the heart of the mirror's cold earth
His form, like a rose, suddenly grew;
His velvet eyes rippled – he was looking at me,
Ah, even in imagination's view

I leaned against the wall's breast,
Softly I said, "Is this you, Kami?"
But I saw that from the bitter past
Naught but a name remained to me

عاقبت خط جاده پایان یافت
من رسیدم ز ره غبار آلود
تشنه بر چشمه ره نبرد و دریغ
شهر من گور آرزویم بود

The ribbon of the road ended at last,
Covered with dust I arrived;
Thirsty, I could not reach the spring. Alas!
My town was a grave to my desire

بعد ها

مرگ من روزی فرا خواهد رسید:
در بهاری روشن از امواج نور
در زمستانی غبار آلود و دور
یا خزانی خالی از فریاد و شور

مرگ من روزی فرا خواهد رسید:
روزی از این تلخ و شیرین روزها
روز پوچی همچو روزان دگر
سایه‌ای ز امروزها، دیروزها!

دیدگانم همچو دالانهای تار
گونه‌هایم همچو مرمرهای سرد
ناگهان خوابی مرا خواهد ربود
من تهی خواهم شد از فریاد درد

میخزند آرام روی دفترم
دستهایم فارغ از افسون شعر
یاد میآرم که در دستان من
روز گاری شعله میزد خون شعر

خاك میخواند مرا هر دم به خویش
میرسند از ره که در خاکم نهند
آه شاید عاشقانم نیمه شب
گل بروی گور غمناکم نهند

بعد من ناگه به یکسو میروند
پرده‌های تیره دنیای من
چشمهای ناشناسی میخزند
روی کاغذها و دفترهای من

Afterwards

One day my death will come
In a spring awash with waves of light
In a winter misty, far from sight
Or an autumn void of cries of passions bright

One day my death will come,
From among these sweet and bitter days,
An empty day like all the rest
A shadow of today's and yesterdays

My eyes like dim-lit hallways,
My cheeks like marbles, cold as stone;
Suddenly a sleep will seize me,
I will be empty of shouts and woe

Over my notebooks slowly creep
My hands now free of poetry's spell;
I recall, once in these hands
There flamed the blood of poetry

Dust calls me every moment to itself,
They come and pause to place me in my grave;
My lovers, ah, at midnight will perhaps
Lay roses upon my grieving grave

The dark veils of my world suddenly
Are lifted after me.
The eyes of strangers will creep
Upon my papers and notebooks.

در اتاق کوچکم پا مینهد
بعد من، با یاد من بیگانه‌ای
در بر آئینه میماند بجای
تارموئی، نقش دستی، شانه‌ای

مي رهم از خویش و میمانم ز خویش
هر چه بر جا مانده ویران میشود
روح من چون بادبان قایقی
در افقها دور و پنهان میشود

میشتابند از پی هم بی شکیب
روزها و هفته‌ها و ماهها
چشم تو در انتظار نامه‌ای
خیره میماند بچشم راهها

لیك دیگر پیکر سرد مرا
میفشارد خاك دامنگیر خاك!
بی تو، دور از ضربه‌های قلب تو
قلب من میپوسد آنجا زیر خاك

بعد ها نام مرا باران و باد
نرم میشویند از رخسار سنگ
گور من گمنام میماند به راه
فارغ از افسانه‌های نام و ننگ

مونیخ زمستان 1958

When I am gone, in my little room
A stranger to my memory will stand;
In the mirror's bosom there remains
A hair, a comb, the imprint of a hand.

I am freed, from myself I stand apart,
Destruction falls on all that remains;
My spirit like the sail of a sea-borne ship
Fades on the horizon and then wanes.

Days and weeks and months, impatiently
Upon each other's footsteps hasten by;
Expecting soon a letter, staring wide,
You eyes remain fixed on the roadway.

But now the clinging dust of earth,
Upon my stone-cold body presses firm;
Without you, far from your beating heart,
My heart decays there beneath that earth.

Afterwards the rain and gentle breeze
Will wash my name off from the face of the stone;
By the road my grave will be unnamed,
Free of tales that speak of fame and shame.

Munich, Winter 1958

آورد به اضطرارم اوّل بوجود
جز حیرتم از حیات چیزی نفزود
رفتیم به اکراه وندانیم چه بود؟
زین آمدن بودن و رفتن مقصود
"خیّام"

بندگی

برلبانم سایه‌ای از پرسشی مرموز
دردلم دردیست بی آرام و هستی سوز
راز سر گردانی این روح عاصی را
با تو خواهم در میان بگذاردن، امروز

گرچه از درگاه خود میرانیم اما
تا من اینجا بنده، تو آنجا، خدا باشی
سر گذشت تیره من، سر گذشتی نیست
کز سر آغاز و سرانجامش جدا باشی

نیمه شب گهواره ها آرام میجنبند
بی خبر از کوچ درد آلود انسانها
دست مرموزی مرا چون زورقی لرزان
میکشد پاروزنان در کام توفانها

چهره‌هائی در نگاهم سخت بیگانه
خانه‌هائی بر فرازش اشك اخترها
وحشت زندان و برق حلقه زنجیر
داستانهائی زلطف ایزد یکتا!

سینه سرد زمین ولکه های گور
هر سلامی سایه تاریك بدرودی
دستهائی خالی و در آسمانی دور
زردی خورشید بیمار تب آلودی

Into existence, helpless first, He fostered me
Adding nothing in life but my perplexity.
Having left reluctantly we never see
In this coming, living, leaving, what purpose there might be.

~Omar Khayyam

Servitude 1[*]

On my lips a mysterious question casts a shade,
In my heart lies a restless and life-burning pain,
The bewildered secret of this rebellious soul
I want to put forth with you today.

Though from your threshold you banish me, yet as long
As I am here, servant, and you are there, God,
My dark dismal story shall not be a tale
In whose beginning and end you remain apart

At midnight the cradles rock peacefully,
Unaware of the painful migration of man;
Like a quivering boat in the mouth of a storm
I am drawn by an unknown mysterious hand.

Faces before my eyes gravely foreign,
Houses atop which fall the stars' tears,
Fear of prison and the flashing of chains,
Tales of the grace of the one God so dear!

The cold breast of earth and the gravestone,
Every hello a dark shade's address,
Hands empty and in a distant sky
The sick and fevered yellow of the sun.

---

* The following verses are excerpts from "Servitude I," ~~~ between stanzas indicate where there have been omissions.

جستجوئی بی سرانجام و تلاشی گنگ
جاده ای ظلمانی و پائی به ره خسته
نه نشان آتشی بر قله‌های طور
نه جوابی از ورای این در بسته

آه ... آیا ناله‌ام ره میبرد در تو؟
تا زنی بر سنگ، جام خود پرستی را
یك زمان با من نشینی، بامن خاکی
از لب شعرم بنوشی درد هستی را

* * *

چیستم من؟ زاده یك شام لذتبار
ناشناسی پیش میراند در این راهم
روزگاری پیکری بر پیکری پیچید
من بدنیا آمدم، بی آنکه خود خواهم

کی رهایم کرده ای، تا بادو چشم باز
بر گزینم قالبی، خود از برای خویش؟
تا دهم بر هر که خواهم نام مادر را
خود به آزادی نهم در راه پای خویش

من بدنیا آمدم تا در جهان تو
حاصل پیوند سوزان دو تن باشم
پیش از آن کی، آشنا بودیم ما باهم؟
من بدنیا آمدم بی آنکه «من» باشم

روزها رفتند و در چشمم سیاهی ریخت
ظلمت شبهای کور دیر پای تو
روزها رفتند و آن آوای لالائی
مرد و پرشد گوشهایم از صدای تو

An endless search and a struggle vain,
The road dark and the feet weary of the way,
No sign of fire on the summits of Tur,*
No answer from behind the closed door convey.

Ah…does my lamenting reach you?
To break self-worship's cup upon the stone,
Sit with me, I a mortal, for a time,
And drink life's pain from the lips of my poem.

* * *

What am I? Child of a pleasure-filled night,
A stranger thrusts me on this way;
Once a body entwined around another,
And will-lessly into this world I came.

When did you free me, so I could choose
A form for myself, with two open eyes? –
To name for mother whomever I will,
To set foot on the path without captive ties.

I came into life, in your world to be
The issue of two bodies' burning bond;
When had we known each other before, you and I?
I came into life without being "I".

Days passed and blackness crept into my eyes,
The darkness of your blind and enduring nights
Days passed and my ears filled with your voice
As the song of the lullaby died

---

* Mt. Sinai.

«کودکي» همچون پرستوهای رنگین بال
رو بسوی آسمانهای دگر پر زد
نطفه اندیشه در مغزم بخود جنبید
میهمانی بی خبر انگشت بر در زد

میدویدم در بیابانهای وهم انگیز
می نشستم در کنار چشمه‌ها سرمست
میشکستم شاخه‌های راز را، اما
از تن این بوته هردم شاخه ای میرست

راه من تا دور دست دشتها میرفت
من شناور در شط اندیشه‌های خویش
میخزیدم در دل امواج سر گردان
می گسستم بند ظلمت را زپای خویش

عاقبت روزی ز خود آرام پرسیدم:
چیستم من؟ از کجا آغاز میبابم؟
گر سراپا نور گرم زندگی هستم،
از کدامین آسمان راز میتابم؟

ترس ترسان در پی آن پاسخ مرموز
سر نهادم در رهی تاریك و پیچاپیچ
سایه افکندی بر آن «پایان» و دانستم
پای تاسر هیچ هستم، هیچ هستم، هیچ

سایه افکندی بر آن «پایان» و دردستت
ریسمانی بود و آنسویش بگردنها
میکشیدی خلق را در کوره راه عمر
چشمهاشان خیره در تصویر آن دنیا

میکشیدی خلق را در راه و میخواندی:
آتش دوزخ نصیب کفر گویان باد
هر که شیطان را بجایم بر گزیند او
آتش دوزخ بجانش سخت سوزان باد

"Childhood" flew off toward other skies,
Like swallows of colored wing;
The seed of thought stirred in my mind of itself,
An unannounced guest rapped at the door.

I would run in the deserts of fancy,
Drunken I would sit beside its springs;
I would break the branches of mystery,
Yet each moment a new branch its bush would bring.

My path led to distant fields and plains,
On the tide of my thoughts was I borne;
In the heart of the wandering waves I crept,
From my feet the chains of the dark I tore.

Finally one day I quietly asked:
What am I? From where do I come?
If I am completely the warm light of life,
Which sky of mystery do I radiate from?

Fear followed that secretive answer –
I set out on a dark twisted road;
A shadow you cast on that "end," and I knew
I am nothing, nothing, from head to toe.

A shadow you cast on that "end," and your hand
Held a rope around people's necks;
You were dragging them down life's tortuous path,
While their eyes stared at the other world

You were dragging them down the path, and reciting:
May the fire of hell be the infidels' toll!
Who chooses the devil in place of me,
May the fire of hell burn his soul!

آفریدی خود تو این شیطان ملعون را
عاصیش کردی و او را سوی ما راندی
این تو بودی، این تو بودی، کزیکی شعله
دیوی اینسان ساختی، در راه بنشاندی

چشم ما تا در دو چشم زندگی افتاد
با «خطا» این لفظ مبهم آشنا گشتیم
تو خطا را آفریدی، او بخود جنبید
تاخت برما، عاقبت نفس خطا گشتیم

گر تو با ما بودی ولطف تو با ما بود
هیچ شیطان را بما مهری و راهی بود؟
هیچ در این روح طغیان کرده عاصی
زو نشانی بود، یا آوای پائی بود؟

تو من و ما را پیاپی میکشی در گور
تا بگوئی میتوانی اینچنین باشی
تا من و ما، جلوه گاه قدرتت باشیم
بر سر ما، پتك سرد آهنین باشی

It was you who created this accursed devil,
Turned him rebel and drove him toward us;
It was you, it was you who from a flame
Such a demon made and set on the road.

As soon as our eyes met the eyes of life
We met up with sin,* this ambiguous name;
Sin you created, it moved of itself,
Rushed in upon us, and sin we became.

Would we, were you and your kindness with us,
Leaning or love for the devil know?
Would sign or sound of his footstep still be
In this teaming and raging rebel soul?

You steadily draw me and us into the grave
So you can say, "Thus can I be;"
So that me and us can be the manifestation of your power
You're the cold iron sledge on our head.

---

* Forugh uses the Persian word *khata*, which means error or mistake as opposed to *gonah*, which means sin, but "sin" seems to be closest English word in our understanding of the poem.

آن روزها

آن روزها رفتند
آن روزهای خوب
آن روزهای سالم سرشار
آن آسمان‌های پر از پولك
آن شاخساران پر از گیلاس
آن خانه‌های تکیه داده در حفاظ سبز پیچکها، بیکدیگر

آن بام‌های بادبادکهای بازیگوش
آن کوچه‌های گیج از عطر اقاقی ها

آن روزها رفتند
آن روزهائی کز شکاف پلکهای من
آوازهایم، چون حبابی از هوا لبریز، میجوشید
چشمم به روی هر چه میلغزید
آنرا چو شیر تازه مینوشید
گوئی میان مردمکهایم
خرگوش نا آرام شادی بود
هر صبحدم با آفتاب پیر
به دشتهای ناشناس جستجو میرفت
شبها به جنگل های تاریکی فرو میرفت

آن روزها رفتند
آن روزهای برفی خاموش
کز پشت شیشه، در اتاق گرم،
هر دم به بیرون، خیره میگشتم
پاکیزه برف من، چو کرکی نرم،
آرام میبارید
بر نردبام کهنه چوبی
بر رشته سست طناب رخت
بر گیسوان کاجهای پیر
و فکر میکردم به فردا، آه
فردا-
حجم سفید لیز.

Those Days

Those days are gone
Those fine days
Those sound, abundant days
Those skies filled with spangles
Those cherry-laden branches
Those houses leaning upon each other within green fences of ivy

Those rooftops of frolicking kites
Those alleys giddy with the acacia's perfume

Those days are gone
Those days when my songs burst forth
from between my open eyelids
like bubbles filled with air
Whatever my eyes would glide upon
like fresh milk they would drink
It was as though, within the pupils of my eyes,
there lived a restless rabbit of joy
who every morning, with the ancient sun,
would go in search of unknown fields,
and disappear each night into the woods of darkness.

Those days are gone
Those days of silent snow,
when every moment, in the warm room,
I gazed out through the window pane.
My pure snow, like soft fluff, would quietly drift down
on the old wooden ladder
on the slack clothes-line
on the tresses of the aged pines.
And I'd be thinking of tomorrow, ah
Tomorrow –
a slick white mass.

با خش و خش چادر مادر بزرگ اغاز میشد
و با ظهور سایه مغشوش او، در چار چوب در
- که ناگهان خود را رها میکرد در احساس سرد نور -
و طرح سرگردان پرواز کبوترها
در جامهای رنگی شیشه.
فردا ...

گرمای کرسی خواب آور بود
من تند و بی پروا
دور از نگاه مادرم خطهای باطل را
از مشق های کهنه خود پاك میکردم
چون برف میخوابید
در باغچه میگشتم افسرده
در پای گلدانهای خشك یاس
گنجشگ های مرده‌ام را خاك میکردم

آن روزها رفتند
آن روزهای جذبه و حیرت
آن روزهای خواب و بیداری
آن روزها هر سایه رازی داشت
هر جعبه سر بسته گنجی را نهان میکرد
هر گوشه صندوقخانه، در سکوت ظهر،
گوئی جهانی بود
هر کس ز تاریکی نمی ترسید
در چشمهایم قهرمانی بود

It would begin with the rustle of grandma's veil,
with the appearance of a vague shadow in the frame of the door
– which would suddenly release itself in the cold sensations of light –
and the doves' wandering pattern of flight
etched on the colored window panes
Tomorrow…

The warmth of the korsi* would bring sleep.
I, quickly and heedlessly,
far from my mother's eye,
would erase from my old exercise books the teacher's check marks†
When the snow slept
I would wander, slowly, through the garden
At the foot of the withered jasmine pots
Depressed, I would bury my dead sparrows

Those days are gone
Those days of rapture and wonder
Those days of wakefulness and sleep
Those days when each shadow held a secret,
each sealed box concealed a treasure,
as though each corner of the store-room in the silence of high noon
was a world unto itself.
Anyone not afraid of the dark
was a hero in my eyes

---

* *Korsi:* a heating devise consisting of a low table covered with a large quilt, underneath which lies a brazier filled with red hot coals overlaid with ash. The table is surrounded with mattresses and cushions, and the room is used for sleeping at night and as a living room by day.

† A teacher would draw a line across the page of a child's handwriting exercises to show that he or she had seen it. Students would sometimes attempt to erase this line and re-submit the same exercises.

آن روزها رفتند
آن روزهای عید
آن انتظار آفتاب و گل
آن رعشه‌های عطر
در اجتماع ساکت و محجوب نرگس‌های صحرائی
که شهر را در آخرین صبح زمستانی
دیدار میکردند
آوازهای دوره گردان در خیابان دراز لکه‌های سبز

بازار در بوهای سر گردان شناور بود
در بوی تند قهوه و ماهی
بازار در زیر قدمها پهن میشد، کش میآمد، با تمام
لحظه‌های راه می آمیخت
و چرخ میزد، در ته چشم عروسکها
بازار مادر بود که میرفت با سرعت بسوی حجم
های رنگی سیال
و باز میآمد
با بسته‌های هدیه با زنبیل های پر
بازار باران بود که میریخت، که میریخت،
که میریخت

آن روزها رفتند
آن روزهای خیرگی در رازهای جسم
آن روزهای آشنائی های محتاطانه، با زیبائی رگ
های آبی رنگ
دستی که با يك گل
از پشت دیواری صدا میزد
يك دست دیگر را
ولکه‌های کوچك جوهر، بر این دست مشوش،
مضطرب، ترسان
و عشق،
که در سلامی شرم آگین خویشتن را باز گو میکرد
در ظهرهای گرم دود آلود
ما عشقمان را در غبار کوچه میخواندیم
ما با زبان ساده گلهای قاصد آشنا بودیم

Those days are gone
Those festive days
That expectation of sun and flowers
Those tremulous wafts of perfume
in the shy and silent company of wild narcissus,
which would visit the city
on the last morning of winter.
The rhymes of the roaming peddlers; the long streets with patches of green

The bazaar was afloat with delirious smells,
with the pungent scent of coffee and fish.
The bazaar would expand beneath one's feet,
stretch and mingle with all the moments on the way,
round it would turn in the depths of the eyes of the dolls.
The bazaar was mother who would quickly go
toward the colorful fluid forms
and then return
with boxes of gifts and baskets full.
The bazaar was rain that poured, that poured.

Those days are gone
Those days of wonder at the body's secrets
Those days of cautious acquaintance with the
beauty of bluish veins,
a hand that would call
with a single rose
another hand from behind a wall,
and the little ink spots on this hand –
trembling, anxious, fearful –
and love,
which would repeat itself in a shy hello.
On warm and smoke-filled afternoons
we would sing of our love in the dust of the street,
We were familiar with the simple language of dandelions.*

* In popular belief, dandelions were thought to transmit messages when the sender would blow upon them.

ما قلبهامان را به باغ مهربانی های معصومانه
میبردیم
و به درختان قرض میدادیم
و توپ، با پیغام‌های بوسه در دستان ما میگشت
و عشق بود، آن حس مغشوشی که در تاریکی
هشتی
نا گاه
محصورمان میکرد
وجذبمان میکرد، در انبوه سوزان نفس ها و تپش ها و تبسم‌های دزدانه

آن روزها رفتند
آن روزها مثل نباتاتی که در خورشید میپوسند
از تابش خورشید پوسیدند
و گم شدند آن کوچه‌های گیج از عطر اقاقی ها
در ازدهام پرهیاهوی خیابانهای بی برگشت.
و دختری که گونه‌هایش را
با برگهای شمعدانی رنگ میزد، آه
اکنون زنی تنهاست
اکنون زنی تنهاست

We would take our hearts to the garden of innocent kindness
and loan them to the trees
and the ball, with messages of kisses,
would pass between our hands.
It was love, that vague sensation,
in the darkness of a porch
that suddenly
would surround us,
enrapture us, in the burning flurry of breaths, and heartbeats,
        and stolen smiles

Those days are gone
Those days like plants rotting in the sun,
rotting from the rays of the sun.
Lost are those alleys giddy with acacia's perfume
lost in the clamoring of streets with no return.
And the girl who used to color her cheeks
with the petals of geraniums – ah,
now is a lonely woman,
now is a lonely woman.

گذران

تا به کی باید رفت
از دیاری به دیاری دیگر
نتوانم، نتوانم جستن
هر زمان عشقی و یاری دیگر
کاش ما آن دو پرستو بودیم
که همه عمر سفر میکردیم
از بهاری به بهاری دیگر

آه، اکنون دیریست
که فرو ریخته در من، گوئی،
تیره آواری از ابر گران
چو می آمیزم، با بوسه تو
روی لبهایم، میپندارم
میسپارد جان عطری گذران

آنچنان آلوده ست
عشق غمناکم با بیم زوال
که همه زندگیم میلرزد
چون ترا مینگرم
مثل اینست که از پنجره‌ای
تك درختم را، سرشار از برگ،
در تب زرد خزان مینگرم
مثل اینست که تصویری را
روی جریان‌های مغشوش آب روان مینگرم

شب و روز
شب و روز
شب و روز
بگذار
که فراموش کنم.

Passing

How long must one go
from land to land
I can't, I can't seek always
a new love, a new beloved.
If only we were those two swallows
traveling all our lives from spring to spring.

Ah, it is now a long time ago
that in me there has crumbled, one might say,
a dark wall from the heavy rain
as I mingle with your kiss
upon my lips, I perceive
my soul leaves a fragrance that fades

So tainted with fear of extinction
is my sorrowful love
that my whole life quakes
as I look at you
it is as if
I watch from a window my only tree laden with leaves
in the yellow fever of fall.
It is as if I trace a picture
in the chaotic currents of a flowing stream

Day and night
Day and night
Day and night
Let me
forget.

تو چه هستی، جز یك لحظه، یك لحظه که چشمان مرا میگشاید در
بر هوت آگاهی؟
بگذار
که فراموش کنم.

What are you, but a moment, a moment which opens my eyes
in the desert of awareness?
Let me
forget.

آفتاب میشود

نگاه کن که غم درون دیده‌ام
چگونه قطره قطره آب میشود
چگونه سایه سیاه سر کشم
اسیر دست آفتاب میشود
نگاه کن
تمام هستیم خراب میشود

شراره‌ای مرا به کام میکشد
مرا به اوج میبرد
مرا به دام میکشد
نگاه کن
تمام آسمان من
پر از شهاب میشود

تو آمدی ز دورها و دورها
ز سر زمین عطرها و نورها
نشانده‌ای مرا کنون به زورقی
زعاجها، ز ابرها، بلورها
مرا ببر امید دلنواز من
ببر به شهر شعرها و شورها
به راه پر ستاره میکشانیم
فراتر از ستاره مینشانیم

نگاه کن
من از ستاره سوختم
لبالب از ستارگان تب شدم
چو ماهیان سرخ رنگ ساده دل
ستاره چین برکه های شب شدم

The Sun Shines

Behold! Within my eyes the woes
melting drop by drop,
how my dark defiant shadow
in the sun's hands is captive caught
Behold!
My whole existence into ruin brought.

A single spark consumes me,
transports me to the highest peaks
and in a trap entombs me
Behold!
My whole sky
fills with falling stars.

You came from far, far away,
from lands of light and of perfume
sitting me down, now, in a boat
of ivory, cloud, and crystal hewn
Take me, heart-endearing hope,
to the city where poems and passions flow.
To the star-strewn path you draw me
And beyond the very stars you seat me

Behold!
How the stars have burned me
I was filled with feverish stars
Like naïve and simple goldfish
In the ponds of night I gleaned the stars

چه دور بود پیش از این زمین ما
به این کبود غرفه‌های آسمان
کنون به گوش من دو باره میرسد صدای تو
صدای بال برفی فرشتگان
نگاه کن که من کجا رسیده‌ام
به کهکشان، به بیکران، به جاودان

کنون که آمدیم تا به اوجها
مرا بشوی با شراب موجها
مرا بپیچ در حریر بوسه‌ات
مرا بخواه در شبان دیر پا
مرا دگر رها مکن
مرا از این ستاره‌ها جدا مکن

* * *

نگاه کن که موم شب براه ما
چگونه قطره قطره آب میشود
صراحی سیاه دیدگان من
به لای لای گرم تو
لبالب از شراب خواب میشود
به روی گاهواره‌های شعر من
نگاه کن
تو میدمی و آفتاب میشود

How distant was our earth in times before
to these azure upper reaches of heaven.
Now to my ear there comes once more your voice,
the sound of snowy wings of angels.
Behold where I've reached,
to the galaxy, to the infinite, and to the eternal.

Now that we have reached these heights
wash me in waves of wine,
wrap me in the silk of your kisses,
desire me in the lingering nights.
Do not ever leave me
do not sever me from these stars.

* * *

Behold how upon our path, night's candle
melts drop by drop
The dark decanter of my eyes
through your warming lullaby
is filled with slumber's wine
Upon the cradles of my poetry
Behold!
You breathe, and the sun shines.

روی خاک

هر گز آرزو نکرده‌ام
یك ستاره در سراب آسمان شوم
یا چو روح بر گزیدگان
همنشین خامش فرشتگان شوم
هرگز از زمین جدا نبوده‌ام
با ستاره آشنا نبوده‌ام

روی خاك ایستاده‌ام
با تنم که مثل ساقهٔ گیاه
باد و آفتاب و آب را
میمکد که زندگی کند

بارور ز میل
بارور ز درد
روی خاك ایستاده‌ام
تا ستاره‌ها ستایشم کنند
تا نسیمها نوازشم کنند

* * *

از دریچه‌ام نگاه میکنم
جز طنین یك ترانه نیستم
جاودانه نیستم
جز طنین یك ترانه جستجو نمیکنم
در فغان لذتی که پاکتر
از سکوت ساده غمیست
آشیانه جستجو نمیکنم
در تنی که شبنمیست
روی زنبق تنم

On the Earth

I have never wanted to be
a star in the sky's mirage
or like the soul of the chosen be
the silent companion of angels
I have never been separate from the earth
I have not been familiar with the stars

I have stood on the earth,
my body which, like the stem of a plant,
sucks in wind and water and sun
to live

Burdened with desire
Burdened with pain
I have stood on the earth
so that stars might praise me
and breezes caress me

* * *

Looking out of my window
I am nothing but the echo of a song
I am not eternal
I seek nothing but the echo of a song
In the moans of a pleasure
Purer than the simple silence of woe
I seek no nest
In a body that is dew
Upon the lily of my body.

* * *

بر جدار کلبه‌ام که زندگیست
با خط سیاه عشق
یاد گارها کشیده‌اند
مردمان رهگذر:
قلب تیر خورده
شمع واژگون
نقطه‌های ساکت پریده رنگ
بر حروف در هم جنون
هر لبی که بر لبم رسید
يك ستاره نطفه بست
در شبم که مینشست
روی رود یادگارها
پس چرا ستاره آرزو کنم؟

* * *

این ترانه منست
-- دلپذیر دلنشین
پیش از این نبوده بیش از این

* * *

On the wall of my hut, which is life,
passers-by
have drawn memories
with the black lines of love:
an arrow-pierced heart
an overturned candle
pale, silent dots
on entangled letters of madness
Every lip that reached mine
conceived a star
in my night that sat
upon the river of memories
So why should I covet a star?

* * *

This is my song
– it satisfies and pleases
Before this, it wasn't more than this

باد ما را خواهد برد

در شب کوچك من، افسوس
باد با برگ درختان میعادی دارد
در شب کوچك من دلهره ویرانیست

گوش کن
وزش ظلمت را میشنوی؟
من غریبانه به این خوشبختی مینگرم
من به نومیدی خود معتادم
گوش کن
وزش ظلمت را میشنوی؟

در شب اکنون چیزی میگذرد
ماه سرخست و مشوش
و بر این بام که هر لحظه در او بیم فرو ریختن است
ابرها، همچون انبوه عزاداران
لحظه باریدن را گوئی منتظرند

لحظه‌ای
و پس از آن، هیچ.
پشت این پنجره شب دارد میلرزد
و زمین دارد
باز میماند از چرخش
پشت این پنجره یك نا معلوم
نگران من و تست

ای سرا پایت سبز
دستهایت را چون خاطره‌ای سوزان، در دستان عاشق من بگذار
و لبانت را چون حسی گرم از هستی
به نوازش‌های لبهای عاشق من بسپار
باد ما را با خود خواهد برد
باد ما را با خود خواهد برد

The Wind Will Take Us Away

In my small night, alas
the wind has a date with the leaves of the trees
In my small night there is fear of ruin

Listen
Do you hear the howl of the darkness?
I, like a stranger, look at this good fortune,
addicted to my own despair.
Listen
Do you hear the howl of the darkness?

Something now is passing in the night
The moon is crimson and perturbed
Above this roof, which moment by moment embraces the fear of falling,
clouds appear, like a mourning throng,
to await the moment of rain.

A moment,
then nothing.
Behind this window the night is trembling
and the earth is slackening
its rotation
Behind this window one unknown
is anxiously awaiting you and I.

O you, verdant from head to toe
Put your hands like a burning memory in my loving embrace,
and entrust your lips aglow from life
to my enamoured lips' caresses
The wind will take us away
The wind will take us away

میان تاریکی

میان تاریکی
ترا صدا کردم
سکوت بود و نسیم
که پرده را میبرد
در آسمان ملول
ستاره‌ای میسوخت
ستاره‌ای میرفت
ستاره‌ای میمرد

ترا صدا کردم
ترا صدا کردم
تمام هستی من
چو یك پیاله شیر
میان دستم بود
نگاه آبی ماه
به شیشه‌ها میخورد

ترانه‌ای غمناك
چو دود برمیخاست
ز شهر زنجره‌ها
چو دود میلغزید
به روی پنجره‌ها
تمام شب آنجا
میان سینه من
کسی ز نومیدی
نفس نفس میزد
کسی به پا میخاست
کسی ترا میخواست
دو دست سرد او را
دو باره پس میزد

In the Dark

In the dark
I called you
There was quiet and a breeze
that rustled the drapes.
In the sorrowful sky
a star was burning
a star was falling
a star was dying

I called you
I called you
My entire existence
was like a cup of milk
between my hands.
The blue glances of the moon
brushed the window panes.

A sad song
was rising like smoke
from the city of crickets,
gliding like smoke
over the window panes.
All night long
within my chest
someone panted, panted
in despair.
Someone wanted to rise
Someone wanted you.
Two icy hands
turned her back once again.

تمام شب آنجا
ز شاخه‌های سیاه
غمی فرو میریخت
کسی ز خود میماند
کسی ترا میخواند
هوا چو آواری
به روی او میریخت

درخت کوچك من
به باد عاشق بود
به باد بیسامان

کجاست خانه باد؟
کجاست خانه باد؟

All night long
from the branches of gloom
sadness was pouring down
Someone was falling short of herself
Someone was calling you
Over her, like a crumbling wall,
air came tumbling down.

My little tree
was in love with the wind,
in love with the wandering wind.

Where is the house of the wind?
Where is the house of the wind?

جمعه

جمعهٔ ساکت
جمعهٔ متروك
جمعهٔ چون کوچه‌های کهنه، غم‌انگیز
جمعهٔ اندیشه‌های تنبل بیمار
جمعهٔ خمیازه‌های موذی کشدار
جمعهٔ بی انتظار
جمعهٔ تسلیم

خانهٔ خالی
خانهٔ دلگیر
خانهٔ در بسته بر هجوم جوانی
خانهٔ تاریکی و تصور خورشید
خانهٔ تنهائی و تفأل و تردید
خانهٔ پرده، کتاب، گنجه، تصاویر

* * *

آه، چه آرام و پر غرور گذر داشت
زندگی من چو جویبار غریبی
در دل این جمعه‌های ساکت متروك
در دل این خانه‌های خالی دلگیر
آه، چه آرام و پر غرور گذر داشت ...

Friday

Friday of silence
Friday, deserted
Friday like old, sorrowful streets
Friday of sick, languid thoughts
Friday of long, noxious yawns
Friday without expectation
Friday of resignation.

An empty house
A depressing house
House with doors barred to the onrush of youth
House of darkness and dreams of the sun
House of solitude, divination, and doubt
House of closets, curtains, pictures, and books.

* * *

Ah, how proudly and quietly it passed!
My life, like a strange stream
in the heart of these silent, deserted Fridays
in the heart of these houses, depressing and empty,
Ah, how proudly and quietly it passed…

عروسك کوکی

بیش از اینها، آه، آری
بیش از اینهامیتوان خاموش ماند

میتوان ساعات طولانی
با نگاهی چون نگاه مردگان، ثابت
خیره شد در دود یك سیگار
خیره شد در شکل یك فنجان
در گلی بیرنگ، بر قالی
در خطی موهوم، بر دیوار

میتوان با پنجه‌های خشك
پرده را یکسو کشید و دید
در میان کوچه باران تند میبارد
کودکی با بادبادکهای رنگینش
ایستاده زیر یك طاقی
گاری فرسوده‌ای میدان خالی را
با شتابی پر هیاهو ترك میگوید

میتوان بر جای باقی ماند
در کنار پرده، اما کور، اما کر

میتوان فریاد زد
با صدائی سخت کاذب، سخت بیگانه
«دوست میدارم»
میتوان در بازوان چیره یك مرد
ماده‌ای زیبا و سالم بود
با تنی چون سفره چرمین
با دو پستان درشت سخت
میتوان در بستر یك مست، یك دیوانه، یك ولگرد
عصمت یك عشق را آلود

Mechanical Doll

More than these, ah, yes
more than these, you can keep silent

For long hours you can stare
with a gaze like the gaze of the dead, fixed,
at the smoke of a cigarette
at the shape of a teacup
at a colorless flower in the rug
at an imaginary line upon the wall.

You can, with withered fingers,
draw aside the curtain and see
a heavy rain falling in the alley
a child with his colorful kites
standing in a doorway.
a dilapidated cart clattering off
hastily from the deserted square.

You can stay there standing
by the curtain, as if deaf, as if blind.

You can cry out
in a voice utterly false and strange
"I love – "
You can, in the over-powering arms of a man
be a wholesome and beautiful female.
with a body like a chamois spread
with large firm breasts.
You can, in the bed of a drunk, a vagrant, a fool
defile the chastity of a love.

میتوان با زیرکی تحقیر کرد
هر معمّای شگفتی را
میتوان تنها به حل جدولی پرداخت
میتوان تنها به کشف پاسخی بیهوده دل خوش ساخت
پاسخی بیهوده، آری پنج یا شش حرف

میتوان یك عمر زانو زد
با سری افکنده، در پای ضریحی سرد
میتوان در گور مجهولی خدا را دید
میتوان با سکه‌ای نا چیز ایمان یافت
میتوان در حجره‌های مسجدی پوسید
چون زیارتنامه‌خوانی پیر
میتوان چون صفر در تفریق و جمع و ضرب
حاصلی پیوسته یکسان داشت
میتوان چشم ترا در پیله قهرش
دکمه بیرنگ کفش کهنه‌ای پنداشت
میتوان چون آب در گودال خود خشکید

میتوان زیبائی یك لحظه را با شرم
مثل یك عکس سیاه مضحك فوری
در ته صندوق مخفی کرد
میتوان در قاب خالی مانده یك روز
نقش یك محکوم، یا مغلوب، یا مصلوب را آویخت
میتوان با صورتك‌ها رخنه دیوار را پوشاند
میتوان با نقشهایی پوچ تر آمیخت

میتوان همچون عروسك‌های کوکی بود
با دو چشم شیشه‌ای دنیای خود را دید
میتوان در جعبه‌ای ماهوت
با تنی انباشته از کاه
سالها در لابلای تور و پولك خفت
میتوان با هر فشار هرزه دستی
بی سبب فریاد کرد و گفت
«آه، من بسیار خوشبختم»

You can abase with cleverness
any wondrous riddle.
You can work alone at a crossword puzzle
You can, alone, please the heart by discovering a useless answer
a useless answer, yes, five or six letters.

You can kneel for a lifetime
with head bowed, at the foot of a cold tomb.
You can see God in the grave of one unknown,
find faith in worthless coins.
You can rot in the cubicles of a mosque
like an old reader of pilgrims' prayers.
Like zero in adding, subtracting, multiplying
you can always attain the same result.
You can take your eyes, in the cocoon of their wrath,
for the colorless buttons of a worn-out shoe
You can, like water, dry up in your own ditch.

You can shamefully conceal the beauty of a moment
like some dark, ridiculous instant photo
in the bottom of a trunk.
You can hang in the empty frame of a day
the picture of someone condemned, or conquered, or crucified.
You can conceal the crack in the wall with masks
You can mingle with images even more absurd.

You can be just like a mechanical doll
and view your world with two glass eyes.
You can sleep in a cloth-lined box for years
with a body stuffed with straw
in the folds of lace and sequins.
You can cry out and say for no reason at all
with every lascivious squeeze of a hand:
"Ah, how lucky I am!"

در خیابانهای سرد شهر

من پشیمان نیستم
من به این تسلیم میاندیشم، این تسلیم درد آلود
من صلیب سر نوشتم را
بر فراز تپه‌های قتلگاه خویش بوسیدم

در خیابان‌های سرد شب
جفت‌ها پیوسته با تردید
یکدگر را ترك میگویند
در خیابانهای سرد شب
جز خدا حافظ، خدا حافظ، صدائی نیست

من پشیمان نیستم
قلب من گوئی در آنسوی زمان جاریست
زندگی قلب مرا تکرار خواهد کرد
و گل قاصد که بر دریاچه‌های باد میراند
او مرا تکرار خواهد کرد

آه، میبینی
که چگونه پوست من میدرد از هم؟
که چگونه شیر در رگهای آبی رنگ پستانهای سرد من
مایه میبندد؟
که چگونه خون
رویش غضروفیش را در کمرگاه صبور من
میکند آغاز؟

من تو هستم تو
و کسی که دوست میدارد
و کسی که در درون خود
ناگهان پیوند گنگی باز مییابد
با هزاران چیز غربت بار نا معلوم
و تمام شهوت تند زمین هستم
که تمام آبها را میکشد در خویش
تا تمام دشتها را بارور سازد

In the Cold Streets of Night

I do not regret
I am thinking of this submission, this pain-infused submission
I have kissed the cross of my fate
At the top of my own sacrificial mounds.

In the cold streets of night
Couples are always parting
with hesitation.
In the cold streets of night
There is no sound but "Goodbye, Goodbye."

I do not regret
It is as if my heart were flowing on the other side of time.
Life will repeat my heart,
and the dandelion sailing on the lakes of the breeze,
it too will repeat me.

Ah, do you see
how my skin is bursting
how the milk is congealing in the blue veins
of my cold breasts?
How the blood
is beginning its cartilaginous growth
in my patient womb?

I am you, you
and the one who loves
and the one who finds, suddenly,
a mute alliance within herself
with thousands of unknown, estranging things once more –
I am the ardent passion of the earth
that draws all waters to itself
to make all valleys fertile, rich and green.

گوش کن
به صدای دور دست من
در مه سنگین اوراد سحرگاهی
و مرا ساکت در آئینه‌ها بنگر
که چگونه باز، با ته‌مانده‌های دستهایم
عمق تاریك خوابها را لمس میسازم
و دلم را خالکوبی میکنم چون لکه‌ای خونین
بر سعادتهای معصومانه هستی

من پشیمان نیستم
از من، ای محبوب من، با یك من دیگر
که تو او را در خیابان‌های سرد شب
با همین چشمان عاشق بازخواهی یافت
گفتگو کن
و بیاد آور مرا در بوسه اندوهگین او
بر خطوط مهربان زیر چشمانت

Listen
to the distant voice of my hand
in the heavy mist of pre-dawn incantations.
Look at me in the silent mirrors,
how once again I touch
the dark depths of all dreams with the remnants of my hands,
and tattoo my heart, like a blot of blood,
on the innocent joys of existence.

I do not regret
From me, O my love,
go on to speak with another me
whom again you will find with the same lover's eyes
in the cold streets of night,
and remember me in her sorrowful kisses
on the kind lines beneath your eyes

آیه‌های زمینی

آنگاه
خورشید سرد شد
و برکت از زمین‌ها رفت

و سبزه‌ها به صحراها خشکیدند
و ماهیان به دریاها خشکیدند
و خاك مردگانش را
زان پس به خود نپذیرفت

شب در تمام پنجره‌های پریده رنگ
مانند یك تصور مشکوك
پیوسته در تراکم و طغیان بود
و راهها ادامه خود را
در تیرگی رها کردند

دیگر کسی به عشق نیندیشید
دیگر کسی به فتح نیندیشید
و هیچکس
دیگر به هیچ چیز نیندیشید

در غارهای تنهائی
بیهودگی به دنیا آمد
خون بوی بنگ و افیون میداد
زنهای باردار
نوزادهای بی سر زائیدند
و گاهواره‌ها از شرم
به گورها پناه آوردند

چه روزگار تلخ و سیاهی
نان، نیروی شگفت رسالت را
مغلوب کرده بود
پیغمبران گرسنه و مفلوك
از وعده گاههای الهی گریختند

Earthly Verses

Then
the sun grew cold
and bounty fled the earth

And grasses dried in the fields
and the fish dried in the seas
and the earth no longer took unto herself
the dead

Night was continually rising and surging
like an uncertain notion
in all the pallid windows
and the roads lost their continuance
in darkness

No one thought of love anymore
No one thought of triumph anymore
And no one
thought of anything anymore

In the caverns of loneliness
futility was born
Blood smelled of bhang and opium
Pregnant women gave birth to headless babes
and cradles, in shame,
took refuge in the graves

What black and bitter days!
Bread had conquered
the wondrous power of prophecy
The hungry, destitute prophets,
fled from the sites of divine tryst

و بره‌های گمشده
دیگر صدای هیهی چوپانی را
در بهت دشتها نشنیدند

در دیدگان آینه‌ها گوئی
حرکات و رنگها و تصاویر
وارونه منعکس میگشت
و بر فراز سر دلقکان پست
و چهره و قیح فواحش
یك هاله مقدس نورانی
مانند چتر مشتعلی میسوخت

مرداب‌های الکل
با آن بخارهای گس مسموم
انبوه بی تحرك روشنفکران را
به ژرفنای خویش کشیدند
و موشهای موذی
اوراق زرنگار کتب را
در گنجه‌های کهنه جویدند

خورشید مرده بود
خورشید مرده بود، و فردا
در ذهن کودکان
مفهوم گنگ گمشده‌ای داشت
آنها غرابت این لفظ کهنه را
در مشق‌های خود
با لکه درشت سیاهی
تصویر مینمودند

مردم،
گروه ساقط مردم
دلمرده و تکیده و مبهوت
در زیر بار شوم جسدهاشان
از غربتی به غربت دیگر میرفتند
و میل دردناك جنایت
در دستهایشان متورم میشد

and the lost lambs no longer heard
the sound of the shepherd's "Hey, hey!"
in the bewilderment of the fields.

It seemed in the eyes of mirrors
that images, colors, and motions
were reflected upside down,
and above the heads of lowborn clowns
and harlots' shameless faces
a sacred glowing halo burned
like a parasol aflame.

The swamps of alcohol
with their acrid poison fumes
sucked the intelligentsia's motionless mass
down into their depths,
and pernicious mice
in the old cupboards
gnawed on the gilded pages of books.

The sun was dead
The sun was dead, and tomorrow
held a lost and muted meaning
in the eyes of every child.
In composition books they traced
the strangeness of this old word
with a large black blot.

People,
the fallen band of people,
disheartened, beaten, and dumb,
bore from exile to exile
the unblest burden of their bodies,
while in their hands there swelled
the painful lust for crime

گاهی جرقه ای، جرقهٔ ناچیزی
این اجتماع ساکت بیجان را
یکباره از درون متلاشی میکرد
آنها به هم هجوم میآوردند
مردان گلوی یکدیگر را
با کارد میدریدند
و در میان بستری از خون
با دختران نا بالغ
همخوابه میشدند

آنها غریق وحشت خود بودند
وحس ترسناك گنهکاری
ارواح کور و کودنشان را
مفلوج کرده بود

پیوسته در مراسم اعدام
وقتی طناب دار
چشمان پر تشنج محکومی را
از کاسه با فشار به بیرون میریخت
آنها به خود فرو میرفتند
و از تصور شهوتناکی
اعصاب پیر و خسته‌شان تیر میکشید

اما همیشه در حواشی میدان‌ها
این جانیان کوچك را میدیدی
که ایستاده‌اند
و خیره گشته‌اند
به ریزش مداوم فواره‌های آب

* * *

شاید هنوز هم
در پشت چشم‌های له شده، در عمق انجماد
یك چیز نیم زنده مغشوش
بر جای مانده بود
که در تلاش بی رمقش میخواست
ایمان بیاورد به پاکی آواز آبها

Sometimes a spark, a trifling spark,
would shatter suddenly from within
this silent, soulless league
Men, rushing upon one another,
would rend each other's throats with knives
and sleep with pre-pubescent girls
in beds of blood.

They were drowned in their own fearfulness,
and the dreaded sense of having sinned
had paralyzed
their blind and senseless souls.

Always, in rites of execution,
when the gallows rope
would squeeze from the sockets
a condemned man's convulsing eyes,
they would retreat into themselves
and their old and tired nerves would twinge
with some voluptuous image.

But along the edges of the squares
you would always see these little criminals
standing
and staring
at the steady flow of the fountains.

* * *

Perhaps still
behind those crushed eyes, in their frozen depths,
something half-living and confused
remained
which in the struggle of its last dying breath
wanted to believe in the purity of the water's song

شاید، ولی چه خالی بی پایانی
خورشید مرده بود
و هیچکس نمیدانست
که نام آن کبوتر غمگین
کز قلبها گریخته، ایمانست

* * *

آه، ای صدای زندانی
آیا شکوه یأس تو هرگز
از هیچ سوی این شب منفور
نقبی بسوی نور نخواهد زد؟
آه، ای صدای زندانی
ای آخرین صدای صداها ...

Perhaps, but what infinite emptiness!
The sun was dead,
and no one knew
that the name of the grief-stricken dove
that had flown from the hearts, was "Faith."

* * *

Ah, voice of the prisoner,
will the plaint of your despair
never burrow a way to light
through any side of this despised night?
Ah, voice of the prisoner
O, final voice of all voices...

هدیه

من از نهایت شب حرف میزنم
من از نهایت تاریکی
و از نهایت شب حرف میزنم

اگر به خانه من آمدی برای من ای مهربان چراغ بیار
و یك دریچه که از آن
به ازدحام کوچه خوشبخت بنگرم

The Gift

I speak of the extremity of night
I speak of the extremity of darkness
and of the extremity of night.

If you come to my house, O kind one, bring for me a lamp
and a window through which to look upon
the happy swarming street.

وهم سبز

تمام روز در آئینه گریه میکردم
بهار پنجره‌ام را
به وهم سبز درختان سپرده بود
تنم به پیله تنهائیم نمیگنجید
و بوی تاج کاغذیم
فضای آن قلمرو بی آفتاب را
آلوده کرده بود

* * *

نمي توانستم، دیگر نمي توانستم
صدای کوچه، صدای پرنده‌ها
صدای گمشدن توپ‌های ماهوتی
وهایهوی گریزان کودکان
و رقص بادکنك‌ها
که چون حباب‌های کف صابون
در انتهای ساقه‌ای از نخ صعود میکردند
و باد، باد که گوئی
در عمق گودترین لحظه‌های تیره همخوابگی نفس میزد
حصار قلعه خاموش اعتماد مرا
فشار میدادند
و از شکافهای کهنه، دلم را بنام میخواندند

تمام روز نگاه من
به چشمهای زندگیم خیره گشته بود
به آن دو چشم مضطرب ترسان
که از نگاه ثابت من میگریختند
و چون دروغگویان
به انزوای بی خطر پلکها پناه میآوردند

Green Illusion

I wept in the mirror all day long
Spring had entrusted my window
to the green illusion of the trees
My body could not be contained
in the cocoon of my loneliness
and the smell of my paper crown had polluted
the atmosphere of that sunless scene.

* * *

I could not, I could no longer –
the sound of the street, the sound of the birds,
the sound of tennis balls being lost,
and the fleeing clamour of children,
the dance of balloons, like bubbles of soap,
climbing aloft at the tip of a stem of string,
and the wind, the wind, as if panting
at the bottom of love-making's deepest dark moments,
pressed upon the walls
of the silent citadel of my confidence
and through the ancient fissures
called my heart by name.

All day long my gaze was fixed
upon the eyes of my life,
upon those anxious fearing eyes
that fled from my steady gaze
and took refuge, like liars,
in the safe retreat of eyelids.

کدام قله کدام اوج؟
مگر تمامی این راههای پیچاپیچ
در آن دهان سرد مکنده
به نقطه تلاقی و پایان نمیرسند؟
به من چه دادید، ای واژه‌های ساده فریب
و ای ریاضت اندامها و خواهش‌ها؟
اگر گلی به گیسوی خود میزدم
از این تقلب، از این تاج کاغذین
که بر فراز سرم بو گرفته است، فریبنده تر نبود؟

* * *

چگونه روح بیابان مرا گرفت
و سحر ماه ز ایمان گله دورم کرد!
چگونه نا تمامی قلبم بزرگ شد
و هیچ نیمه‌ای این نیمه را تمام نکرد!
چگونه ایستادم و دیدم
زمین به زیر دو پایم ز تکیه گاه تهی میشود
و گرمی تن جفتم
به انتظاز پوچ تنم ره نمیبرد!

کدام قله کدام اوج؟
مرا پناه دهید ای چراغ‌های مشوش
ای خانه‌های روشن شکاك
که جامه‌های شسته در آغوش دودهای معطر
بر بامهای آفتابیتان تاب میخورند

مرا پناه دهید ای زنان ساده کامل
که از ورای پوست، سر انگشت‌های نازکتان
مسیر جنبش کیف آور جنینی را
دنبال میکند
و در شکاف گریبانتان همیشه هوا
به بوی شیر تازه میآمیزد

Which summit, which peak?
Do not all these winding roads
reach this junction and then end
in that cold and sucking mouth?
What did you give me, O words beguiling the naive,
And O mortification of bodies and desires?
Would it not have been more enticing
to have fixed a rose upon my hair
than all this falsehood, than this paper crown that smells upon my head?

* * *

How I was taken by the spirit of the wild,
and the moon's magic estranged me from the faith of the flock!
How great became the incompleteness of my heart,
and how no half ever made this half whole!
How I stood and watched the earth
sliding from under my feet,
and the warmth of my lover's body
not meeting my body's futile need!

Which summit, which peak?
Give me shelter, O perturbed lamps,
O bright and doubt-filled houses
upon whose sunny roofs
clean clothes flutter in the arms of fragrant smoke.

Give me shelter, O simple perfect women
whose fine and delicate fingertips
trace rapturous embryonic movements
beneath the skin
from the opening of whose shirts
the smell of fresh milk forever mingles with air.

کدام قله کدام اوج؟
مرا پناه دهید ای اجاقهای پر آتش - ای نعل‌های خوشبختی -
و ای سرود ظرفهای مسین در سیاهکاری مطبخ
و ای ترنم دلگیر چرخ خیاطی
و ای جدال روز و شب فرشها و جاروها

مرا پناه دهید ای تمام عشق‌های حریصی
که میل دردناك بقا بستر تصرفتان را
به آب جادو
و قطره‌های خون تازه میآراید

* * *

تمام روز   تمام روز
رها شده، رها شده، چون لاشه‌ای بر آب
به سوی سهمناکترین صخره پیش میرفتم
به سوی ژرفـترین غارهای دریائی
و گوشتخوارترین ماهیان
و مهره‌های نازك پشتم
از حس مرگ تیر کشیدند

نمیتوانستم   دیگر نمیتوانستم
صدای پایم از انکار راه بر میخاست
و یأسم از صبوری روحم وسیعتر شده بود
و آن بهار، و آن و هم سبز رنگ
که بر دریچه گذر داشت، با دلم میگفت
«نگاه کن
تو هیچگاه پیش نرفتی
تو فرو رفتی.»

Which summit, which peak?
Give me shelter, O hearths full of fire –
And O horseshoes of good fortune –
And O song of copper pots and pans in the sooty toil of the kitchen,
And O depressing hum of the sewing machine,
And O constant contention of carpet and broom
Give me shelter, O greedy loves all
whose nuptial beds are adorned by the painful desire for existence
with talismanic water*
and drops of virginal blood

* * *

All day long,   all day long
cast like a corpse on the water, cast,
I moved toward the most frightening rocks,
toward the deepest caverns of the sea
and the most carnivorous fish,
and the slender vertebrae of my back
stiffened with the sense of death

I could not,   I could not any longer –
the sound of my footsteps rose in denial of the road,
my despair had out stepped the patience of my soul,
and that spring, and that green illusion
that passed by the window, said to me
"Look
You never went forward
You went under."

---

* When a man took a second wife, it was important to the first wife that she safeguard her hold upon the man's affections, and to do so she would employ various superstitious devices. One such device was to sprinkle specially prepared water over the nuptial bed of the new bride, a custom to which Forugh refers in this line.

جفت

شب می آید
و پس از شب، تاریکی
و پس از تاریکی
چشمها
دستها
و نفس‌ها و نفس‌ها و نفس‌ها...
و صدای آب
که فرو میریزد قطره قطره قطره از شیر

بعد دو نقطه سرخ
از دو سیگار روشن
تیک تاك ساعت
و دو قلب
و دوتنهائی

Couple

Night falls
and after night, darkness
and after darkness
eyes
hands
and breathing, breathing, breathing…
and the sound of water
dripping from the faucet drop by drop by drop.

Then two red glows
of two lit cigarettes
the tick-tock of the clock
and two hearts
and two solitudes

فتح باغ

آن کلاغی که پرید
از فراز سرما
و فرو رفت در اندیشه آشفته ابری ولگرد
و صدایش همچون نیزه کوتاهی، پهنای افق را پیمود
خبر ما را با خود خواهد برد به شهر

* * *

همه میدانند
همه میدانند
که من و تو از آن روزنه سرد عبوس
باغ را دیدیم
و از آن شاخه بازیگر دور از دست
سیب را چیدیم

همه میترسند
همه میترسند، اما من و تو
به چراغ و آب و آینه پیوستیم
و نترسیدیم

سخن از پیوند سست دو نام
و همآغوشی در اوراق کهنه یك دفتر نیست
سخن از گیسوی خوشبخت منست
با شقایق‌های سوخته بوسه تو
و صمیمیت تن‌هامان، در طراری
و درخشیدن عریانیمان
مثل فلس ماهیها در آب
سخن از زندگی نقره‌ای آوازیست
که سحرگاهان فواره کوچك میخواند

مادر آن جنگل سبز سیال
شبی از خرگوشان وحشی
و در آن دریای مضطرب خونسرد
از صدف‌های پر از مروارید

The Conquest of the Garden

That crow that flew
over our heads
and plunged into the troubled thoughts of a wandering cloud,
whose cry traversed, like a short spear, the expanse of the horizon
will carry news of us to the town.

* * *

Everyone knows
Everyone knows
that you and I saw the garden
from that tiny window, cold and stern
and picked the apple from that frolicking branch
beyond our grasp.

Everyone is fearful
Everyone is fearful, but you and I
joined the water and mirror and light
and were not afraid.

The talk is not of a loose bond between two names
nor of an embrace in a registry's old pages
The talk is of my lucky hair
with the burning peonies of your kiss,
of our candid bodies in playfulness,
the iridescence of our nakedness
like the scales of fish in water
The talk is of the silvery life of a song
that the little fountain sings at dawn.

In that green and rippling forest
we asked one night the wild hares,
in that restless and indifferent sea
we asked the pearl-laden shells,

و در آن کوه غریب فاتح
از عقابان جوان پرسیدیم
که چه باید کرد

همه میدانند
همه میدانند
ما به خواب سرد و ساکت سیمرغان، ره یافته‌ایم
ما حقیقت را در باغچه پیدا کردیم
در نگاه شرم‌آگین گلی گمنام
و بقا را در یك لحظه نا محدود
که دو خورشید به هم خیره شدند

سخن از پچ پچ ترسانی در ظلمت نیست
سخن از روزست و پنجره‌های باز
و هوای تازه
و اجاقی که در آن اشیاء بیهده میسوزند
و زمینی که ز کشتی دیگر بارور است
و تولد و تکامل و غرور
سخن از دستان عاشق ماست
که پلی از پیغام عطر و نور و نسیم
بر فراز شبها ساخته‌اند

به چمنزار بیا
به چمنزار بزرگ
و صدایم کن، از پشت نفس‌های گل ابریشم
همچنان آهو که جفتش را

پرده‌ها از بغضی پنهانی سرشارند
و کبوترهای معصوم
از بلندیهای برج سپید خود
به زمین مینگرند

and on that forlorn, triumphant mountain
we asked the young eagles
what should be done?

Everyone knows
Everyone knows
that we've found a way to the cold and silent sleep of the phoenixes
that we discovered truth in the garden
in the shy glance of a nameless flower
and found existence in one infinite moment
when two suns gazed at one another.

The talk is not of a fearful whisper in the dark
The talk is of day and open windows
and fresh air,
of a hearth upon which useless things burn
of a land sown with a different seed
of birth, evolution, and pride
The talk is of our loving hands
that over the nights have built a bridge
from the message of fragrance, and breezes, and light.

Come to the meadow
Come to the great meadow
and call me from behind the breath of acacia blossoms
just as the deer calls its mate.

The curtains are filled with a hidden sorrow,
and from the heights of their white towers
innocent doves
cast eyes upon the ground.

گل سرخ

گل سرخ
گل سرخ
گل سرخ

او مرا برد به باغ گل سرخ
و به گیسوهای مضطربم در تاریکی گل سرخی زد
و سر انجام
روی برگ گل سرخی با من خوابید

ای کبوترهای مفلوج
ای درختان بی تجربه یائسه. ای پنجره‌های کور،
زیر قلبم در اعماق کمر گاهم، اکنون
گل سرخی دارد میروید
گل سرخ
سرخ
مثل يك پرچم در
رستاخیز

آه، من آبستن هستم، آبستن، آبستن

Red Rose

Red rose
Red rose
Red rose

He took me to the garden of red roses
and in the darkness he placed a red rose
in my trembling hair
Finally, he slept with me on the petal of a red rose.

O paralyzed pigeons
O untried, menopausal trees, O blind windows
Beneath my heart, in the depths of my womb, now
a red rose is growing
red rose
red
like a flag on
Resurrection Day.

Ah, I am pregnant, pregnant, pregnant.

پرنده فقط یك پرنده بود

پرنده گفت: «چه بوئی، چه آفتابی، آه
بهار آمده است
و من به جستجوی جفت خویش خواهم رفت.»

پرنده از لب ایوان
پرید، مثل پیامی پرید و رفت

پرنده کوچك بود
پرنده فکر نمیکرد
پرنده روزنامه نمیخواند
پرنده قرض نداشت
پرنده آدمها را نمیشناخت

پرنده روی هوا
و بر فراز چراغهای خطر
در ارتفاع بی خبری میپرید
و لحظه‌های آبی را
دیوانه وار تجربه میکرد

پرنده، آه، فقط یك پرنده بود

The Bird Was Only a Bird

"Ah, what fragrance, what sun!" said the bird
"Spring has come,
"I will go seek my mate."

The bird flew off the veranda's edge,
it flew like a message and hastened away

The bird was small
The bird didn't think
He read no papers
nor had any loans.
The bird did not know people.

In the air
above the red lights of danger
in the heights of oblivion the bird flew
and experienced madly
the moments of azure blue.

The bird, ah, was only a bird.

ای مرز پر گهر

فاتح شدم
خود را به ثبت رساندم
خود را به نامی، در یك شناسنامه، مزین کردم
و هستیم به یك شماره مشخص شد
پس زنده باد 678 صادره از بخش 5 ساکن تهران
دیگر خیالم از همه سو راحتست
آغوش مهربان مام وطن
پستانك سوابق پر افتخار تاریخی
لالائی تمدن و فرهنگ
و جق و جق جقجقه قانون ...
آه
دیگر خیالم از همه سو راحتست

از فرط شادمانی
رفتم کنار پنجره، با اشتیاق، ششصد و هفتاد و هشت بار
هوا را که از اغبار پهن
و بوی خاکروبه و ادرار، منقبض شده بود
درون سینه فرو دادم
و زیر ششصد و هفتاد و هشت قبض بدهکاری
و روی ششصد و هفتاد و هشت تقاضای کار نوشتم
فروغ فرخزاد

در سرزمین شعر و گل بلبل
موهبتیست زیستن، آنهم
وقتی که واقعیت موجود بودن تو پس از سال‌های سال پذیرفته میشود
جائی که من
با اولین نگاه رسمیم از لای پرده، ششصد وهفتاد وهشت شاعر را میبینم
که، حقه بازها، همه در هیئت غریب گدایان
در لای خاکروبه، به دنبال وزن و قافیه میگردند
و از صدای اولین قدم رسمیم

O Bejewelled Land

I did it
I got myself registered
dressed myself up in an ID card with a name
and my existence was distinguished by a number
So long live 678, issued by precinct 5, resident of Tehran.
Now my mind is completely at ease
The kind bosom of motherland
the nipple of former ages full of history's glory
the lullaby of culture and civilization
and the rattling of the rattle of the law…
Ah
Now my mind is completely at ease

With utmost joy
I walked to the window and fervently, six-hundred
seventy-eight times, drew into my breast
air grown thick
with the dust of dung and the stench of garbage and urine
And at the bottom of six-hundred seventy-eight IOU's,
atop six-hundred seventy-eight job applications, I wrote
        Forugh Farrokhzad

In the land of poetry, nightingales, and roses
living is a blessing, yes, indeed
when the fact of your being, after so many years, is approved –
a place where I
with my first official glance see six-hundred seventy-eight poets
      through the folds of the curtain
impostors, each in the strange guise of beggars
searching for rhymes and meters in heaps of rubbish
And from the sound of my first official step

یکباره، از میان لجن‌زارهای تیره، ششصد و هفتاد و هشت بلبل مرموز
که از سر تفنن
خود را بشکل ششصد و هفتاد و هشت کلاغ سیاه پیر در آورده‌اند
با تنبلی بسوی حاشیه روز میپرند
و اولین نفس زدن رسمیم
آغشته میشود به بوی ششصد و هفتاد و هشت شاخه گل سرخ
محصول کارخانجات عظیم پلاسکو

موهبتیست زیستن، آری
در زادگاه شیخ ابودلقك کمانچه کش فوری
و شیخ ای دل ای دل تنبك تبار تنبوری
شهر ستارگان گران وزن ساق و باسن و پستان و پشت جلد هنر
گهواره مؤلفان فلسفه «ای بابا به من چه ولش کن»
مهد مسابقات المپیك هوش - وای!
جائی که دست به هر دستگاه نقلی تصویر و صوت میزنی، از آن
بوق نبوغ نابغه‌ای تازه سال می آید
و برگزیدگان فکری ملت
وقتی که در کلاس اکابر حضور میيابند
هر یك به روی سینه، ششصد و هفتاد و هشت کباب پز برقی
و بر دو دست، ششصد و هفتاد و هشت ساعت ناوزر ردیف کرده و میدانند
که ناتوانی از خواص تهی کیسه بودنست، نه نادانی

فاتح شدم بله فاتح شدم
اکنون به شادمانی این فتح
در پای آینه، با افتخار، ششصد و هفتاد و هشت شمع نسیه میافروزم
و میپرم به روی طاقچه تا با اجازه، چند کلامی

suddenly, from the dark and slimy marshes, six-hundred seventy-eight
mysterious nightingales
who have donned for fun the form of six-hundred
seventy-eight old black crows
flap lazily off toward the edge of day.
And my first official breath
is imbued with the smell of six-hundred seventy-eight red rose stems,
product of the great PLASCO* factories

Living is a blessing, yes
in the home of Sheikh Fool-son, instant fiddler
and Sheikh O-Heart-Heart of the drum, clan of drums,
city of superstar champions – legs, hips, breasts and glossy cover art,
cradle of the authors of the philosophy, "Hey man, what's it to me,"
source of Olympic quiz-show games – ay!
a place where from every broadcast you turn on, in vision or voice,
there blares the bleating horn of some young ingenious genius,
and the nation's intellectual elite
when they gather in literacy† classes
each has arranged upon his breast six-hundred seventy-eight electric
kebab grills
and on each wrist six-hundred seventy-eight Navzer‡ watches, and they
know
that impotence comes from an empty purse, not from ignorance

I've done it, yes I've done it
Now to celebrate this victory
I proudly light, at the foot of the mirror, six-hundred seventy-eight
charge-account candles
and leap to the ledge to deliver, by your leave,

* PLASCO was the largest plastic factory in Iran at the time.
† In Iran, under the Shah, because the literacy rate was near 47%, attending literacy classes was becoming typical.
‡ A popular Swiss watch at that time, often given out as a prize on radio quiz shows.

در باره فواید قانونی حیات به عرض حضورتان برسانم
و اولین کلنگ ساختمان رفیع زندگیم را
همراه با طنین کف زدنی پرشور
بر فرق فرق خویش بکوبم

من زنده‌ام، بله، مانند زنده رود، که یکروز زنده بود
و از تمام آنچه که در انحصار مردم زنده ست، بهره خواهم برد

من میتوانم از فردا
در کوچه‌های شهر، که سرشار از مواهب ملیست
و در میان سایه‌های سبکبار تیرهای تلگراف
گردش کنان قدم بردارم
و با غرور، ششصد و هفتاد و هشت بار، به دیوار
مستراح‌های عمومی بنویسم
خط نوشتم که خر کند خنده

من میتوانم از فردا
همچون وطن پرست غیوری
سهمی از ایده‌آل عظیمی که اجتماع
هر چارشنبه بعد از ظهر، آنرا
با اشتیاق و دلهره دنبال میکند
در قلب و مغز خویش داشته باشم
سهمی از آن هزار هوس پرور هزار ریالی
که میتوان به مصرف یخچال و مبل و پرده رساندش
یا آنکه در ازای ششصد و هفتاد و هشت رأی طبیعی
آنرا شبی به ششصد و هفتاد و هشت مرد وطن بخشید

a few words on the legal advantages of life
And strike the first blow of the pick-axe for building the lofty edifice of my life
to resounding, thunderous applause
right on top of my head

I am living; yes, like the Zendehrud River,* which once lived too,
and I'll take my share from all that exists in the monopoly of living men.

From tomorrow on I shall be able
to walk along, strolling
through the city's streets abounding in national blessings,
through the shadows of unburdened telegraph poles,
and I'll write, six-hundred and seventy-eight times, proudly
on public toilet walls:
I wrote this line to make asses laugh

From tomorrow on I shall be able
to hold in heart and mind
like any zealous patriot
a share of that profound ideal everyone pursues
passionately and anxiously
each Wednesday afternoon –
a share of those thousand fantasies born of each thousand-Rial bill†
that you can redeem for curtains, furniture or fridge
or give some night, in exchange for six-hundred seventy-eight natural votes
to six-hundred seventy-eight sons of the native land‡

---

* "Zendeh Rud," a river in Isfahan. The name means "the river of life," but since it is only a seasonal river, it is often completely dry.

† Reference to a national charity organization headed by one of the Shah's sisters which sponsored a lottery every Wednesday. The prize was 100,000 tumans (= one million rials). The times were one of low economic productivity, and everyone would wait until 4 p.m. Wednesday for the announcement of the winner. The winner would receive one-thousand thousand-rial notes.

‡ Reference to the practice of buying votes on the part of those seeking to be elected to the Parliament.

من میتوانم از فردا
در پستوی مغازه خاچیك
بعد از فرو کشیدن چندین نفس، ز چند گرم جنس
دست اول خالص
و صرف چند بادیه پپسی کولای نا خالص
و پخش چند یا حق و یاهو و وغوغ و هوهو
رسماً به مجمع فضلای فکور و فضله‌های فاضل روشنفکر
و پیروان مکتب داخ داخ تاراخ تاراخ بپیوندم
و طرح اولین رمان بزرگم را
که در حوالی سنه یکهزار و ششصد و هفتاد و هشت شمسی تبریزی
رسماً به زیر دستگاه تهی دست چاپ خواهد رفت
بر هر دو پشت ششصد و هفتاد و هشت پاکت
اشنوی اصل ویژه بریزم

من میتوانم از فردا
با اعتماد کامل
خود را برای ششصد و هفتاد و هشت دوره به یك دستگاه مسند مخمل پوش
در مجلس تجمع و تأمین آتیه
یا مجلس سپاس و ثنا میهمان کنم
زیرا که من تمام مندرجات مجله هنر و دانش - و تملق و کرنش را میخوانم
و شیوه «درست نوشتن» را میدانم
من در میان توده سازنده‌ای قدم به عرصه هستی نهاده‌ام
که گر چه نان ندارد، اما بجای آن
میدان دید باز و وسیعی دارد
که مرزهای فعلی جغرافیائیش

From tomorrow on I'll be able
in the back room of Khachik's store
after taking a few snorts from some grams
of pure first-rate stuff,
and drinking a few glasses of impure Pepsi
and reciting a few O-God's, Praise-be's, croak-croak's and
coo-coo's
to officially join the congregation of learned scholars and the offals
of enlightened intellectuals
and the disciples of the blah-blah blabber-blabber school
And the draft of my first great novel
will officially go to the bankrupt press
around the Shamsi-Tabrizi year one-thousand six-hundred and
seventy-eight*
scrawled out on both sides of six-hundred seventy-eight packs
of special genuine Oshnu cigarettes.

From tomorrow on I'll be able
to invite myself with complete aplomb
to six-hundred seventy-eight sessions of a velvet-couched
organization
in the assembly for gathering and guaranteeing the future
or the assembly for thanksgiving and praise –
for I've read from cover to cover the journal of Art and learning,
and the journal of Homage and Flattery
and I know the style of "good writing"
I have set foot on the field of existence amid the creative masses
which having no bread have nevertheless
a broad and open field of vision,
the actual geographical bounds of which

---

* There are two calendars in the Moslem world, one lunar and one solar, both dating from *Hejrat,* ie., from the date of Mohammad's flight from Mecca to Medina. The lunar calendar is "Hejri qamari" and the solar "Hejri shamsi." Forugh changes it here to "shamsi tabrizi," thus calling to mind Shams-e Tabriz, Jalaleddin Rumi's friend and muse.

از جانب شمال، به میدان پر طراوت و سبز تیر
و از جنوب، به میدان باستانی اعدام
و در مناطق پر ازدحام، به میدان توپخانه رسیده ست
و در پناه آسمان درخشان و امن امنیتش
از صبح تا غروب، ششصد و هفتاد و هشت قوی قوی هیکل گچی
به اتفاق ششصد و هفتاد و هشت فرشته
- آنهم فرشته از خاك و گل سرشته - به تبلیغ طرحهای سکون و سکوت مشغولند

فاتح شدم   بله فاتح شدم
پس زنده باد 678 صادره از بخش 5 ساکن تهران
که در پناه پشتکار و اراده
به آنچنان مقام رفیعی رسیده است، که در چار چوب پنجره‌ای
در ارتفاع ششصد و هفتاد وهشت متری سطح زمین قرار گرفته ست

و افتخار این را دارد
که میتواند از همان دریچه - نه از راه پلکان - خود را
دیوانه وار به دامان مهربان مام وطن سرنگون کند
و آخرین وصیتش اینست
که در ازای ششصد و هفتاد و هشت سکه، حضرت
استاد آبراهام صهبا
مرثیه‌ای به قافیه کشك در رثای حیاتش رقم زند

extend in the north to the verdant greenery of Target Square*
and in the south, to ancient Execution Square†
and in the center of town, to Cannon Square‡
And in the shelter of their shining skies,
in their utter safeness,
six-hundred seventy-eight immense plaster swans
in alliance with six-hundred seventy-eight angels – they too made
of earth and clay –
busy themselves from dawn to dusk launching plans for stillness
and silence

I've done it,   yes, I've done it
So long live 678, issued from precinct 5, resident of Tehran,
who in the shelter of perseverance and will
has attained so high a standing as to have settled down on a
window sill
six-hundred and seventy-eight meters above the ground
And she has this honor –
to cast herself headlong from her perch – not by the stairs –
madly into motherland's kind lap
And her last wish is this,
that in return for six-hundred seventy-eight coins
the great master Abraham Sahba§
exalt her life with an elegy that ends in nonsensical rhymes.

---

* A square north of Tehran used for military target practice. It is also used occasionally as a place for executing political dissidents.

† A square south of Tehran which was once used for public hangings of common criminals.

‡ A square in downtown Tehran which was occasionally used in the past for hangings.

§ Ebrahim Sahba, a third-rate poet associated with the Iran-American Society. Forugh deridingly changes his name here to the Americanized "Abraham." Sahba would typically write occasional poetry about insignificant events.

به آفتاب سلامی دوباره خواهم داد

به آفتاب سلامی دوباره خواهم داد
به جویبار که در من جاری بود
به ابرها که فکرهای طویلم بودند
به رشد دردناك سپیدارهای باغ که با من
از فصل‌های خشك گذر میکردند
به دسته‌های کلاغان
که عطر مزرعه‌های شبانه را
برای من هدیه میآوردند
به مادرم که در آئینه زندگی میکرد
و شکل پیری من بود
و به زمین، که شهوت تکرار من، درون ملتهبش را
از تخمه‌های سبز میانباشت - سلامی، دوباره خواهم داد

میآیم، میآیم، میآیم
با گیسویم: ادامه بوهای زیر خاك
با چشمهایم: تجربه‌های غلیظ تاریکی
با بوته‌ها که چیده‌ام از بیشه‌های آنسوی دیوار
میآیم، میآیم، میآیم
و آستانه پر از عشق میشود
و من در آستانه به آنها که دوست میدارند
و دختری که هنوز آنجا،
در آستانه پر عشق ایستاده، سلامی دوباره خواهم داد

I Will Greet the Sun Once Again

I'll give greetings to the sun once again,
to the stream that flowed within me,
to the clouds that were my tallest thoughts,
to the painful growth of aspens in the garden
that endured the seasons of drought with me,
to the flock of crows
who as a gift
brought the fields' nocturnal scent to me,
to my mother who lived in the mirror
and revealed the figure of my old age,
and to the earth, whose burning womb I've filled
with green seeds in my lust for repetition – I'll give greetings once
    again.

I come, I come, I come
with my hair exuding the smells beneath the earth
with my eyes, thick with experiences of gloom
with the bouquet of greens I picked from the wood, on the other
    side of the wall
I come, I come, I come
The threshold fills with love
and I, on the threshold, will greet once again
those who love, and the girl
still standing on the threshold filled with love.

تولدی دیگر

همهٔ هستی من آیه تاریکیست
که ترا در خود تکرار کنان
به سحر گاه شگفتن‌ها و رستن‌های ابدی خواهد برد
من در این آیه ترا آه کشیدم، آه
من در این آیه ترا
به درخت و آب و آتش پیوند زدم

* * *

زندگی شاید
یك خیابان درازاست که هر روز زنی با زنبیلی از آن
میگذرد
زندگی شاید
ریسمانیست که مردی با آن خود را از شاخه میآویزد
زندگی شاید طفلیست که از مدرسه بر میگردد

زندگی شاید افروختن سیگاری باشد، در فاصله
رخوتناك دو همآغوشی
یا عبور گیج رهگذری باشد
که کلاه از سر بر میدارد
و به یك رهگذر دیگر با لبخندی بی معنی میگوید
«صبح بخیر»
زندگی شاید آن لحظه مسدودیست
که نگاه من در نی نی چشمان تو خود را ویران میسازد
و در این حسی است
که من آنرا با ادراك ماه و با دریافت ظلمت خواهم
آمیخت

در اتاقی که باندازه یك تنهائیست
دل من
که به اندازه یك عشقست
به بهانه‌های ساده خوشبختی خود مینگرد
به زوال زیبای گل‌ها در گلدان
به نهالی که تو در باغچه خانه‌مان کاشته‌ای
و به آواز قناریها
که به اندازه یك پنجره میخوانند

Another Birth

All my existence is a dark verse
which repeating you in itself will take you
to the dawn of eternal blossoming and growth
I have sighed to you in this verse, ah,
in this verse I have grafted you
to tree and water and fire.

* * *

Perhaps life
is a long street on which a woman with a basket passes every day.
Perhaps life
is a rope with which a man hangs himself from a branch.
Perhaps life is a child returning from school.

Perhaps life is lighting a cigarette in the languid repose
    between two embraces
or the mindless transit of a passer-by
who tips his hat
and with a meaningless smile says "good morning" to another passer-by.
Perhaps life is that thwarted moment
when my gaze destroys itself in the pupil of your eyes.
And in this lies a sensation
which I will mingle with the perception of the moon and the discovery
    of darkness.

In a room the size of one loneliness
my heart
the size of one love
looks at the simple pretexts of its happiness,
at the fading of the beauty of the flowers in the vase
at the sapling you planted in the garden of our house
at the song of the canaries
that sing the size of one window

آه ...
سهم من اینست
سهم من اینست
سهم من
آسمانیست که آویختن پرده‌ای آنرا از من میگیرد
سهم من پائین رفتن از یك پله متروکست
و به چیزی در پوسیدگی و غربت واصل گشتن
سهم من گردش حزن آلودی در باغ خاطره‌هاست
و در اندوه صدائی جان دادن که به من میگوید:
«دستهایت را
دوست میدارم»

دستهایم را در باغچه میکارم
سبز خواهم شد، میدانم، میدانم، میدانم
و پرستوها در گودی انگشتان جوهریم
تخم خواهند گذاشت

گوشواری به دو گوشم میآویزم
از دو گیلاس سرخ همزاد
و به ناخن‌هایم برگ گل کوکب میچسبانم
کوچه‌ای هست که در آنجا
پسرانی که به من عاشق بودند، هنوز
با همان موهای درهم و گردن های باریك و پاهای لاغر
به تبسم های معصوم دخترکی میاندیشند که یکشب او را
باد با خود برد

کوچه‌ای هست که قلب من آنرا
از محله‌های کودکیم دزدیده‌ست

Ah…
This is my lot
This is my lot
My lot
is a sky which the hanging of a curtain steals from me.
My lot is descending an abandoned stair
to find something in decay and exile.
My lot is a grief-stricken walk in the garden of memories
and surrendering my soul in the sadness of a voice that says to me:
"I love
your hands"

I plant my hands in the garden
I will grow green, I know, I know, I know
and in the hollows of my ink-stained fingers
swallows will lay eggs

On my ears I hang earrings of twin red cherries
and stick dahlia petals on my nails*
There is a street where
still, the boys who loved me
with the same toussled hair, slender necks, lanky legs
think of the innocent smile of a girl
whom one night the wind took away

There is a street which my heart
has stolen from the scenes of my childhood

---

* Young girls would put flower petals on their fingernails to imitate the nail polish of grown-up women.

سفر حجمی در خط زمان
و به حجمی خط خشك زمان را آبستن کردن
حجمی از تصویری آگاه
که زمهمانی یك آینه بر میگردد
و بدینسانست
که کسی میمیرد
و کسی میماند

هیچ صیادی در جوی حقیری که به گودالی میریزد،
مرواریدی صید نخواهد کرد

من
پری کوچك غمگینی را
میشناسم که در اقیانوسی مسکن دارد
و دلش را در یك نی لبك چوبین
مینوازد آرام، آرام
پری کوچك غمگینی
که شب از یك بوسه میمیرد
و سحر گاه از یك بوسه به دنیا خواهد آمد

The journey of a form on the line of time
and with a form, impregnating the barren line of time,
a form aware of an image
which returns from the party of a mirror.
And it is thus
that someone dies
and someone remains

In the shallow stream that flows into a ditch,
    no fisherman will hunt a pearl.

I
know a sad little fairy
who settles in the ocean
and plays her heart on a wood-tipped flute
softly, softly
a sad little fairy
who dies from a single kiss at night
and will be born with a single kiss at dawn.

ایمان بیاوریم به آغاز فصل سرد

و این منم
زنی تنها
در آستانهٔ فصلی سرد
در ابتدای درك هستی آلودهٔ زمین
و یأس ساده و غمناك آسمان
و ناتوانی این دستهای سیمانی

زمان گذشت
زمان گذشت و ساعت چهار بار نواخت
چهار بار نواخت
امروز روز اول دیماه است
من راز فصل ها را میدانم
و حرف لحظه ها را میفهمم
نجات دهنده در گور خفته است
و خاك، خاك پذیرنده
اشارتیست به آرامش

زمان گذشت و ساعت چهار بار نواخت.

در کوچه باد می آید
در کوچه باد می آید
و من به جفت گیری گل ها میاندیشم
به غنچه هایی با ساق های لاغر کم خون
و این زمان خستهٔ مسلول
و مردی از کنار درختان خیس میگذرد
مردی که رشته‌های آبی رگهایش
مانند مارهای مرده از دو سوی گلوگاهش
بالا خزیده‌اند
و در شقیقه‌های منقلبش آن هجای خونین را تکرار میکنند:

Let Us Believe in the Beginning of a Cold Season

And this is me
a lonely woman
on the threshold of a cold season
at the beginning of perceiving a contaminated existence
    of the earth
and the simple and sad despair of the heavens
and the impotence of these concrete hands.

Time passed
Time passed and the clock struck four times
It struck four times
Today is the first day of winter*
I know the secrets of the seasons
and understand the words of the moments.
The savior is asleep in the grave
and the dust, the receiving dust
is an indication of quiet.

Time passed and the clock struck four times.

In the street the wind is blowing
In the street the wind is blowing
and I think of the pollination of the flowers
of the buds with thin anemic stems
and this tired, consumptive time
A man is passing by the wet trees
a man, the lines of whose bluish veins
have crept up both sides of his throat
like dead snakes
and in his throbbing temples those sanguine syllables are repeated:

---

* Literally the line reads: "Today is the first day of the month of *Day*." *"Day"* is the tenth month of the solar Iranian calendar, and marks the beginning of winter.

- سلام
- سلام
و من به جفت گیری گل‌ها مي انديشم.

در آستانهٔ فصلی سرد
در محفل عزای آینه‌ها
و اجتماع سوگوار تجربه‌های پریده رنگ
و این غروب بارور شده از دانش سکوت
چگونه میشود به آنکسی که میرود اینسان
صبور،
سنگین،
سرگردان،
فرمان ایست داد.
چگونه میشود به مرد گفت که او زنده نیست، او هیچوقت
زنده نبوده‌ست

در کوچه باد می آید
کلاغهای منفرد انزوا
در باغ‌های پیر کسالت میچرخند
و نردبام
چه ارتفاع حقیری دارد.

آنها تمام ساده لوحی يك قلب را
با خود به قصر قصه‌ها بردند
و اکنون دیگر
دیگر چگونه یکنفر به رقص بر خواهد خاست
و گیسوان کودکیش را
در آب‌های جاری خواهد ریخت
و سیب را که سر انجام چیده است و بوئیده است
در زیر پا لگد خواهد کرد؟

ای یار، ای یگانه ترین یار
چه ابرهای سیاهی در انتظار روز میهمانی خورشیدند.

– hello
– hello
and I think of the pollination of the flowers.

On the threshold of a cold season,
in the mournful assembly of mirrors
in the dirgeful gathering of pale experiences
in this sunset impregnated with the knowledge of silence
how can one order a person to stop
who travels
so patiently
so gravely
so lost?
How can one tell a man he's not alive, that he's never
    been alive?

In the street the wind is blowing
lonely crows of isolation
circle around the old gardens of indolence
and the ladder,
how low is its height.

They took all the credulity of a heart with them
    to the castle of legends
and now, once more,
how will a person rise once more to dance
and cast the tresses of her childhood
upon the flowing waters
and trample the apple underfoot
that she has finally picked and smelled?

O friend, O most singular friend,
what dark clouds await the day of the party of the sun!

انگار در مسیری از تجسم پرواز بود که یکروز آن پرنده نمایان شد
انگار از خطوط سبز تخیل بودند
آن برگ‌های تازه که در شهوت نسیم نفس میزدند
انگار
آن شعلهٔ بنفش که در ذهن پاك پنجره‌ها میسوخت
چیزی بجز تصور معصومی از چراغ نبود.

در کوچه باد مي آید
این ابتدای ویرانیست
آن روز هم که دست های تو ویران شدند باد می آمد
ستاره‌های عزیز
ستاره‌های مقوائی عزیز
وقتی در آسمان، دروغ وزیدن میگیرد
دیگر چگونه میشود به سوره‌های رسولان سرشکسته پناه آورد؟
ما مثل مرده‌های هزاران هزار ساله به هم میرسیم و آنگاه
خورشید بر تباهی اجساد ما قضاوت خواهد کرد.

من سردم است
من سردم است و انگار هیچوقت گرم نخواهم شد
ای یار ای یگانه ترین یار «آن شراب مگر چند ساله بود؟»
نگاه کن که در اینجا
زمان چه وزنی دارد
و ماهیان چگونه گوشت‌های مرا میجوند
چرا مرا همیشه در ته دریا نگاه میداری؟

من سردم است و از گوشواره‌های صدف بیزارم
من سردم است و میدانم
که از تمامی اوهام سرخ یك شقایق وحشی
جز چند قطره خون
چیزی بجا نخواهد ماند.

It's as if in the course of an envisioned flight one day that bird appeared
It's as if those new leaves that were breathing in the passion of the breeze
were verdant lines of imagination.
It's as if the violet flame burning
in the pure mind of the windows
was nothing but the innocent illusion of the lamp.

In the street the wind is blowing
This is the beginning of ruination.
That day when your hands were ruined the wind was blowing too
    O beloved stars
    O beloved cardboard stars
when lies begin to blow in the skies
how can one take refuge anymore in the verses of disgraced prophets?
We, like the dead of thousands of years ago, reach each other, and then
shall preside over the destruction of our bodies.

I am cold
I am cold, as if I'll never be warmed
O friend, O most singular friend, how old was that wine anyway?
Look what a weight
time has here
and how the fish chew my flesh
Why do you always keep me at the bottom of the sea?

I am cold, and weary of shell earrings
I am cold, and know
that nothing will remain from all the red illusions of a wild peony*
except a few drops of blood.

---

* The wild peony often connotes revolutionaries who have been killed, much like "stars" in a poem such as "My Heart Grieves for the Garden."

خطوط را رها خواهم کرد
و همچنین شمارش اعداد را رها خواهم کرد
و از میان شکل‌های هندسی محدود
به پهنه‌های حسی وسعت پناه خواهم برد
من عریانم، عریانم، عریانم
مثل سکوت‌های میان کلام‌های محبت عریانم
و زخم‌های من همه از عشق است
از عشق، عشق، عشق.
من این جزیرهٔ سرگردان را
از انقلاب اقیانوس
و انفجار کوه گذر داده‌ام
و تکه تکه شدن، راز آن وجود متحدی بود
که از حقیر ترین ذره‌هایش آفتاب به دنیا آمد.

سلام ای شب معصوم!

سلام ای شبی که چشم‌های گرگ‌های بیابان را
به حفره‌های استخوانی ایمان و اعتماد بدل میکنی
و در کنار جویبارهای تو، ارواح بیدها
ارواح مهربان تبرها را میبویند
من از جهان بی تفاوتی فکرها و حرف‌ها و صداها میآیم
و این جهان به لانهٔ ماران مانند است
و این جهان پر از صدای حرکت پاهای مردمیست
که همچنان که ترا میبوسند
در ذهن خود طناب دار ترا می بافند

سلام‌ای شب معصوم!

میان پنجره و دیدن
همیشه فاصله ایست
چرا نگاه نکردم؟
مانند آن زمان که مردی از کنار درختان خیس گذرمیکرد ...

I will let go of the lines
and likewise let go the counting of numbers
from the midst of defined geometrical forms
I will seek refuge in the tangible spaces of vastness
I am naked, naked, naked
naked like the moments of silence between the phrases of love
And my wounds are all due to love
from love, love, love.
I have guided this wandering island
through the tumults of the ocean,
through the eruption of mountains,
and shattering was the secret of that unified existence
from whose most humble particles the sun was born.

Greetings, O innocent night!

Greetings, O night who changes the eyes of desert wolves
into bony sockets of faith and trust,
by the side of whose streams the spirits of willows
smell the kind spirits of axes
I come from the indifferent world of thoughts and words and voices
and this world resembles snake holes
this world resounds with the footsteps of people
who while they kiss you
weave for you a gallows's rope in their minds.

Greetings, O innocent night!

Between the window and the seeing
always lies a distance.*
Why did I not look?
Like that time when a man was passing by the wet trees…

---

* Cf. T.S. Eliot in "The Hollow Men": "Between the idea and the act/Falls the shadow."

چرا نگاه نکردم؟
انگار مادرم گریسته بود آنشب
آنشب که من به درد رسیدم و نطفه شکل گرفت
آنشب که من عروس خوشه‌های اقاقی شدم
آنشب که اصفهان پر از طنین کاشی آبی بود،
و آنکسی که نیمهٔ من بود، به درون نطفهٔ من باز گشته بود
و من در آینه میدیدمش،
که مثل آینه پاکیزه بود و روشن بود
و ناگهان صدایم کرد
و من عروس خوشه‌های اقاقی شدم ...
انگار مادرم گریسته بود آنشب.
چه روشنائی بیهوده‌ای در این دریچهٔ مسدود سرکشید
چرا نگاه نکردم؟
تمام لحظه‌های سعادت میدانستند
که دست‌های تو ویران خواهد شد
و من نگاه نکردم

تا آن زمان که پنجرهٔ ساعت
گشوده شد و آن قناری غمگین چهار بار نواخت
چهار بار نواخت
و من به آن زن کوچك بر خوردم
که چشمهایش، مانند لانه‌های خالی سیمرغان بودند
و آنچنان که در تحرك رانهایش میرفت
گوئی بکارت رؤیای پرشکوه مرا
با خود بسوی بستر شب میبرد.

آیا دو باره گیسوانم را
در باد شانه خواهم زد؟
آیا دوباره باغچه ها را بنفشه خواهم کاشت؟
و شمعدانی ها را
در آسمان پشت پنجره خواهم گذاشت؟
آیا دو باره روی لیوان ها خواهم رقصید؟
آیا دو باره زنگ در مرا بسوی انتظار صدا خواهد برد؟

Why did I not look?
It was as if my mother had wept that night,
that night when I felt the pain and the seed was conceived
that night when I became the bride of acacia blossoms
that night when Isfahan abounded with the echoes of blue tiles,
and that man who was my mate had returned within my seed*
I could see him in the mirror
He was clean and bright like the mirror
Suddenly he called me
and I became the bride of acacia blossoms...
It was as if my mother had wept that night.
What futile light rose up in this closed and tiny window!
Why did I not look?
All the moments of happiness knew
that your hands would be ruined
and I did not look
until the time when the clock's window opened
and that sad canary struck four times
he struck four times
and I ran into that little woman
whose eyes were like the empty nests of phoenixes
and she walked with such a motion in her thighs
that you'd think she was carrying to the bed of night
the virginity of my glorious dream.

Will I once again comb
my hair in the wind?
Will I once again plant violets in the gardens?
And set geraniums
against the sky behind the window panes?
Will I once again dance on the glasses?
Will the doorbell once again carry me to the expectation of a call?

---

* Possibly a reference to the husband being "renewed" in the image of the son.

به مادرم گفتم: «دیگر تمام شد»
گفتم: «همیشه پیش از آنکه فکر کنی اتفاق میافتد
باید برای روزنامه تسلیتی بفرستیم»

انسان پوك
انسان پوك پر از اعتماد
نگاه کن که دندانهایش
چگونه وقت جویدن سرود میخوانند
وچشمهایش
چگونه وقت خیره شدن میدرند
و او چگونه از کنار درختان خیس میگذرد:
صبور،
سنگین،
سرگردان،

در ساعت چهار
در لحظه‌ای که رشته‌های آبی رگهایش
مانند مارهای مرده از دو سوی گلوگاهش
بالاخزیده‌اند
و در شقیقه‌های منقلبش آن هجای خونین را
تکرار میکنند
- سلام
- سلام
آیا تو
هرگز آن چهار لالهٔ آبی را
بوئیده‌ای؟ ...

زمان گذشت
زمان گذشت و شب روی شاخه‌های لخت اقاقی افتاد
شب پشت شیشه‌های پنجره سر میخورد
و با زبان سردش
ته مانده‌های روز رفته را به درون میکشد

I told my mother: "It's all over now"
I said: "It always happens before you think,
We must put our condolence notice in the paper"

Hollow men
Hollow men filled with confidence
Look how while chewing
his teeth sing a song
and while staring
his eyes are torn
and he, how he passes by the wet trees:
patiently,
gravely,
lost.

At the hour of four
at the moment when the lines of his bluish veins
have crept up both sides of his throat
like dead snakes
and those sanguine syllables are repeated
in his throbbing temples:
– hello
– hello
have you
ever smelled those four
    blue tulips?...*

Time passed
Time passed, and night fell upon the bare acacia branches
Night was slipping behind the window panes
And with its cold tongue
sucking in the last remainders of the vanished day

---

* "Blue tulips" also can refer to lamps with blue crystal or blue glass tops (cf. end of poem).

من از کجا میآیم؟
من از کجا میآیم؟
که اینچنین به بوی شب آغشته‌ام؟
هنوز خاك مزارش تازه ست
مزار آن دو دست سبز جوان را میگویم ...

چه مهربان بودی ای یار، ای یگانه ترین یار
چه مهربان بودی وقتی دروغ میگفتی
چه مهربان بودی وقتی که پلك‌های آینه‌ها را میبستی
وچلچراغ ها را
از ساقه‌های سیمی میچیدی
و در سیاهی ظالم مرا بسوی چراگاه عشق میبردی
تا آن بخار گیج که دنبالهٔ حریق عطش بود بر چمن خواب مینشست

و آن ستاره‌های مقوایی
به گرد لایتناهی میچرخیدند.

چرا کلام را به صدا گفتند؟
چرا نگاه را به خانهٔ دیدار میهمان کردند!
چرا نوازش را
به حجب گیسوان با کِرگی بردند؟
نگاه کن که در اینجا
چگونه جان آنکسی که با کلام سخن گفت
و بانگاه نواخت
و با نوازش از رمیدن آرمید
به تیرهای توهم
مصلوب گشته است
و جای پنج شاخهٔ انگشتهای تو
که مثل پنج حرف حقیقت بودند
چگونه روی گونه او ماندهست.

Where do I come from?
Where do I come from,
that I have become so filled with the smell of night?
The dust of his grave is still fresh
I mean the dust of those two green and youthful hands.

How kind you were, O friend, O most singular friend
How kind you were when you spoke lies
How kind when you closed the eyelids of the mirror
and plucked the lights of the chandelier
off from their wire stems
And in the oppressive darkness you took me to the pastures of love
until that giddy mist which followed upon the fire of thirst would
settle on the meadow of sleep

and those cardboard stars
would spin around infinity.

Why was the word voiced?
Why was looking made a guest in the house of seeing?
Why was caressing taken
to the shyness of virginal hair?
Look how here
the soul of a man
who spoke with a glance
and caressed with a glance
and rested from flight with caresses
has been crucified
on the poles of illusion.
And how there remains upon his cheek
the imprint of the five branches of your fingers, which were like the
five letters of truth.

سکوت چیست، چیست، چیست ای یگانه ترین یار؟
سکوت چیست بجز حرف های ناگفته
من از گفتن میمانم، اما زبان گنجشگان
زبان زندگی جمله‌های جاری جشن طبیعتست.
زبان گنجشگان یعنی: بهار. برگ. بهار.
زبان گنجشگان یعنی: نسیم. عطر. نسیم.
زبان گنجشگان در کارخانه می میرد.

این کیست این کسی که روی جادهٔ ابدیت
بسوی لحظهٔ توحید میرود
و ساعت همیشگیش را
با منطق ریاضی تفریق ها و تفرقه ها کوك میکند.
این کیست این کسی که بانگ خروسان را
آغاز قلب روز نمیداند
آغاز بوی ناشتایی میداند
این کیست این کسی که تاج عشق به سر دارد
و در میان جامه‌های عروسی پوسیده ست؟

پس آفتاب سرانجام
در یك زمان واحد
بر هر دو قطب نا امید نتابید.
تو از طنین کاشی آبی تهی شدی

و من چنان پرم که روی صدایم نماز میخوانند ...

جنازه‌های خوشبخت
جنازه‌های ملول
جنازه‌های ساکت متفکر
جنازه‌های خوش بر خورد، خوش پوش، خوش خوراك
در ایستگاههای وقت های معین
و در زمینهٔ مشکوك نورهای موقت
و شهوت خرید میوه‌های فاسد بیهودگی ...
آه،
چه مردمانی در چار راهها نگران حوادثند

What is silence? – What? What? O most singular friend?
What is silence but unspoken words
I refrain from speaking, but the tongue of sparrows
is the language of life in the flowing sentences of nature's celebration.
The language of sparrows: Spring. Leaf. Spring.
The language of sparrows: Breeze. Fragrance. Breeze.
In factories the language of sparrows dies.

Who is this, this person who walks upon the path of eternity
toward the moment of unity
and with the mathematical logic of subtractions and discords
winds her eternal watch?
Who is this person who does not regard the rooster's crow
as the start of the heart of day
but rather considers it to begin with the smell of breakfast?
Who is this person who wears love's crown upon her head
and has rotted inside the wedding dress?

So the sun did not shine, after all,
upon both poles of hopelessness
in one single instant.
You were emptied of the echoes of blue tiles.

And I am so full that they recite prayers upon my voice…

Happy corpses
despondent corpses
silent, thoughtful corpses
well-mannered, well-dressed and well-eating corpses
in the station of scheduled times
and the dubious background of temporary lights
and the lust for buying the rotten fruits of futility…
Ah,
how people stare at accidents at the intersections

و این صدای سوت‌های توقف
در لحظه‌ای که باید، باید، باید
مردی به زیر چرخ‌های زمان له شود
مردی که از کنار درختان خیس میگذرد ...

من از کجا میآیم؟

به مادرم گفتم: «دیگر تمام شد»
گفتم: «همیشه پیش از آنکه فکر کنی اتفاق میافتد
باید برای روزنامه تسلیتی بفرستیم.»

سلام ای غرابت تنهائی
اتاق را به تو تسلیم میکنم
چرا که ابرهای تیره همیشه
پیغمبران آیه‌های تازه تطهیرند
و در شهادت يك شمع
راز منوری است که آنرا
آن آخرین و آن کشیده ترین شعله خوب میداند.

ایمان بیاوریم
ایمان بیاوریم به آغاز فصل سرد
ایمان بیاوریم به ویرانه‌های باغ های تخیل
به داس های واژگون شدهٔ بیکار
و دانه های زندانی
نگاه کن که چه برفی میبارد ...

شاید حقیقت آن دو دست جوان بود، آن دو دست جوان
که زیر بارش یکریز برف مدفون شد
و سال دیگر، وقتی بهار
با آسمان پشت پنجره همخوابه میشود
و در تنش فوران میکنند
فواره‌های سبز ساقه‌های سبکبار
شکوفه خواهد داد ای یار، ای یگانه ترین یار

and the sound of the traffic-whistles to stop
at the instant that a man must, must, must be
crushed beneath the wheels of time
the man passing beside the wet trees …

Where do I come from?

I told my mother: "It's all over now"
I said:"It always happens before you think
We must put our condolence notice in the paper."

Greetings, O estrangement of loneliness
I surrender the room to you
Why is it always the dark clouds
that are the prophets of new verses of purification?
And in the martyrdom of a candle
there lies a luminous secret
known by that final and tallest flame.

Let us believe
Let us believe in the beginning of a cold season
Let us believe in the ruins of imagination's gardens
in the idle and overturned sickles
and the imprisoned seeds.
Look how the snow is falling …

Perhaps the truth was those two young hands,
those two young hands that were buried beneath the continuous
falling snow
and next year, when the spring
makes love with the sky behind the window
and in its body there bursts forth
green fountains of frolicking stems
they will blossom, O friend, O most singular friend

ایمان بیاوریم به آغاز فصل سرد ...

* * *

ای هفت سالگی
ای لحظهٔ شگفت عزیمت
بعد از تو هر چه وقت، در انبوهی از جنون و جهالت رفت

بعد از تو پنجره که رابطه‌ای بود سخت زنده و روشن
میان ما و پرنده
میان ما و نسیم
شکست
شکست
شکست

بعد از تو آن عروسك خاکی
که هیچ چیز نمیگفت. هیچ چیز بجز آب، آب، آب
در آب غرق شد.

بعد از تو ما صدای زنجره ها را کشتیم
و بصدای زنگ، که از روی حرف های الفبا بر میخاست
و به صدای سوت کارخانه ها، دل بستیم.

بعد از تو که جای بازیمان زیر میز بود
از زیر میزها
به پشت میزها
و از پشت میزها
به روی میزها رسیدیم
و روی میزها بازی کردیم
و باختیم، رنگ ترا باختیم، ای هفت سالگی.

Let us believe in the beginning of a cold season …

* * *

O age of seven*
O moment of wonder at departure
After you, whatever has song, has gone
In a throng of madness and ignorance, it has gone.

After you, the window which had been a luminous and fully living
connection
between us and the bird
between us and the breeze
broke
broke
broke
After you, that clay doll
which said nothing, nothing but water, water, water
was in the water drowned.

After you, we killed the sound of the crickets
and became enamoured with the sound of bells
which rose from the letters of the alphabet
and to the sound of the factory whistles.

After you, our playground was beneath the table,
from beneath the tables
to behind desks
and from behind desks
we reached the table tops
and we played upon the tables
and we lost, we lost your color, O age of seven.

---

* The second part of this poem is unfinished in the original and in places incomplete.

بعد از تو ما به هم خیانت کردیم
بعد از تو ما تمام یادگاري ها را
با تکه هاي سرب ، و با قطره هاي منفجر شدهٔ خون
از گیجگاه هاي گچ گرفتهٔ دیوارهای کوچه زدودیم .

بعد از تو ما به میدان ها رفتیم
و داد کشیدیم :
"زنده باد
مرده باد "

و در هیاهوي میدان ، براي سکه های کوچک آوازه خوان
که زیرکانه به دیدار شهر آمده بودند ، دست زدیم .

بعد از تو ما که قاتل یکدیگر بودیم
برای عشق قضاوت کردیم
و همچنان که قلب هامان
در جیب هایمان نگران بودند
برای سهم عشق قضاوت کردیم

بعد از تو ما به قبرستان ها رو آوردیم
و مرگ، زیر چادر مادر بزرگ نفس میکشید
و مرگ، آن درخت تناور بود
که زنده‌های اینسوی آغاز
به شاخه‌های ملولش دخیل می بستند
و مرده های آنسوی پایان
به ریشه های فسفریش چنگ می زدند
و مرگ روی آن ضریح مقدس نشسته بود
که در چهار زاویه‌اش، ناگهان چهار لالهٔ آبی
روشن شدند.

صدای باد میآید
صدای باد میآید، ای هفت سالگی

After you, we betrayed each other
After you, all our mementos were wiped off
with lead and drops of exploded blood
from the plastered temples of the walls in the street

After you, we went to the squares
and shouted:
"Long live…
"Death to…"

And in the clamor of the square, we clapped for the small,
singing coins
that were visiting the city by subterfuge.

After you, we who were each other's killers
judged for the sake of love
and just as our hearts
were concerned for our pockets
we judged our share of love.

After you, we turned to the graveyards
and death was breathing beneath grandmother's veil
and death was that massive tree
upon whose weary branches
the living on this side of beginning were tying talismans*
and around whose phosphorous roots
there clung the dead on that side of finality
and death was sitting atop that holy shrine
in whose four corners, suddenly,
four blue crystal lamps were lit.

The sound of the wind is coming
the sound of the wind is coming, O age of seven

---

* In villages, people look upon very large and ancient trees with reverence, and fasten ribbons to them in hopes that their problems will be solved.

برخاستم و آب نوشیدم
و ناگهان به خاطر آوردم
که کشتزارهای جوان تو از هجوم ملخ ها چگونه ترسیدند
چقدر باید پرداخت
چقدر باید
برای رشد این مکعب سیمانی پرداخت؟

ما هر چه را که باید
از دست داده باشیم، از دست داده‌ایم
ما بی چراغ به راه افتادیم
و ماه، ماه، مادهٔ مهربان، همیشه در آنجا بود
در خاطرات کودکانهٔ یك پشت بام کاهگلی
و بر فراز کشتزارهای جوانی که از هجوم ملخ ها میترسیدند

چقدر باید پرداخت؟ ...

I rose and took a drink of water
and suddenly I recalled
how your young plantations feared the locusts' swarm.
How much must one pay
How much must one pay
for the growth of this cube of concrete?

Whatever we must give up
we have already given up
We have set out on the road without a lamp
and the moon, the moon, the kind female, was always there
in the childhood memories of a mud thatched rooftop
above the young plantations that feared the locusts' swarm

How much must one pay?

پنجره

يك پنجره براى ديدن
يك پنجره براى شنيدن
يك پنجره كه مثل حلقهٔ چاهى
در انتهاى خود به قلب زمين ميرسد
و باز مى شود بسوى وسعت اين مهربانى مكرر آبى رنگ
يك پنجره كه دست‌هاى كوچك تنهايى را
از بخشش شبانهٔ عطر ستاره‌هاى كريم
سر شار ميكند
و مى شود از آنجا
خورشيد را به غربت گل‌هاى شمعدانى مهمان كرد
يك پنجره براى من كافيست

***

من از ديار عروسك ها ميآيم
از زير سايه هاى درختان كاغذى
در باغ يك كتاب مصور
از فصل‌هاى خشك تجربه‌هاى عقيم دوستى و عشق
در كوچه‌هاى خاكى معصوميت
از سال‌هاى رشد حروف پريده رنگ الفبا
در پشت ميزهاى مدرسهٔ مسلول
از لحظه‌اى كه بچه ها توانستند
بر روى تخته حرف «سنگ» را بنويسند
و سارهاى سراسيمه از درخت كهنسال پر زدند.
من از ميان ريشه هاى گياهان گوشتخوار ميآيم
و مغز من هنوز
لبريز از صداى وحشت پروانه ايست كه او را
در دفترى به سنجاقى
مصلوب كرده بودند.

***

Window

A window for seeing
A window for hearing
A window which like the shaft of a well
extends in its depths to the heart of the earth
and opens toward the expanse of this blue and recurring kindness.
A window that fills the little hands of loneliness
with the nocturnal gift of
the generous stars' perfume
From there one can invite the sun
to the estranged geraniums
One window is enough for me.

***

I come from the land of dolls,
from beneath the shadows of paper trees
in a picture-book garden,
from the dry seasons of barren encounters with friendship and love
in the dusty streets of innocence,
from years of learning the pallid letters of the alphabet
behind the desks of consumptive schools,
from the moment when the children could spell
the word "stone" upon the board
and the starlings flurried off headlong from the aged tree*
I come from amongst the roots of carnivorous plants
and my mind, still,
is brimming with the terrified cry of a butterfly
that they crucified
in a notebook with a pin

---

* "The starlings flew from the trees" is one of the first sentences children learn in their first-grade reader.

وقتی که اعتماد من از ریسمان سست عدالت آویزان بود
و در تمام شهر
قلب چراغ های مرا تکه تکه میکردند.
وقتی که چشم‌های کودکانهٔ عشق مرا
با دستمال تیرهٔ قانون میبستند
و از شقیقه‌های مضطرب آرزوی من
فواره‌های خون به بیرون میپاشید
وقتی که زندگی من دیگر
چیزی نبود، هیچ چیز بجز تیک تاك ساعت دیواری
دریافتم، باید. باید. باید.
دیوانه وار دوست بدارم.

يك پنجره برای من کافیست
يك پنجره به لحظهٔ آگاهی و نگاه و سکوت
اکنون نهال گردو
آنقدر قد کشیده که دیوار را برای برگ‌های جوانش
معنی کند
از آینه بپرس
نام نجات دهنده‌ات را
آیا زمین که زیر پای تو می لرزد
تنها تر از تو نیست؟
پیغمبران ، رسالت ویرانی را
با خود به قرن ما آوردند
این انفجارهای پیاپی
و ابرهای مسموم،
آیا طنین آیه‌های مقدس هستند؟
ای دوست، ای برادر، ای همخون
وقتی به ماه رسیدی
تاریخ قتل عام گل‌ها را بنویس.

When my confidence was dangling from the feeble rope of justice
and all through the city
they shattered the heart of my lamps
When they bound the childish eyes of my love
with the dark handkerchief of the law,
and streams of blood spurted forth from the tremulous temples of
    my desire
When my life was nothing anymore,
nothing but the tick-tock of a clock on the wall
I realized I must, I must, I must
                                        love madly.

A window is enough for me,
a window for a moment of awareness, and seeing, and silence
Now the sapling walnut tree
has grown so tall that it explains
the meaning of "wall" to its young leaves.
Ask the name of your savior
from the mirror
Isn't the earth that trembles beneath your feet
lonelier than you?
The prophets brought with them to our age
a message of destruction
These constant explosions
and poisoned clouds,
are they the echoes of holy verses?
O friend, O brother, O fellow man,
when you reach the moon
inscribe the date of the massacre of the flowers

همیشه خواب ها
از ارتفاع ساده لوحی خود پرت میشوند و می میرند
من شبدر چهار پری را می بویم
که روی گور مفاهیم کهنه روئیده ست
آیا زنی که در کفن انتظار و عصمت خود خاك شد
جوانی من بود؟
آیا دو باره من از پله‌های کنجکاوی خود بالا خواهم رفت
تا به خدای خوب، که در پشت بام خانه قدم می زند سلام بگویم؟

حس میکنم که وقت گذشته ست
حس میکنم که «لحظه» سهم من از برگ های تاریخ است
حس میکنم که میز فاصلهٔ کاذبیست در میان
گیسوان من و دست‌های این غریبهٔ غمگین
حرفی به من بزن
آیا کسی که مهربانی یك جسم زنده را بتو میبخشد
جز درك حس زنده بودن از تو چه میخواهد؟
حرفی به من بزن
من در پناه پنجره‌ام
با آفتاب رابطه دارم

Dreams are thrown, always,
from the heights of their credulity, and die
I smell a four-leaf clover
which has grown upon the grave of outworn values.
Was the woman that turned to dust
In the shroud of her purity and expectation my youth?
Will I again climb the stairs of my curious imagination
to greet the kind God who treads upon our roof?

I feel that time has passed
I feel that "the moment" is my share of the pages of history
I feel that the table is a false space
between my hair and the hands of this sorrowful stranger
Say something to me
Someone who gives you the kindness of a living body,
what does she want from you but the sensation of being alive?
Say something to me
I am in the shelter of the window
I am connected with the sun

دلم برای باغچه میسوزد

کسی به فکر گل‌ها نیست
کسی به فکر ماهیها نیست
کسی نمیخواهد
باور کند که باغچه دارد میمیرد
که قلب باغچه در زیر آفتاب ورم کرده است
که ذهن باغچه دارد آرام آرام
از خاطرات سبز تهی می شود
و حس باغچه انگار
چیزی مجردست که در انزوای باغچه پوسیده ست.

حیاط خانهٔ ما تنهاست
حیاط خانهٔ ما
در انتظار بارش یك ابر ناشناس
خمیازه می کشد
و حوض خانهٔ ما خالی ست
ستاره‌های کوچك بی تجربه
از ارتفاع درختان به خاك میافتند
و از میان پنجره های پریده رنگ خانهٔ ماهی ها
شب ها صدای سرفه میآید
حیاط خانهٔ ما تنهاست.

پدر میگوید:
«از من گذشته ست
از من گذشته ست
من بار خود را بردم
و کار خود را کردم»
و در اتاقش، از صبح تا غروب،
یا شاهنامه میخواند

My Heart Grieves for the Garden

No one is thinking of the flowers
No one is thinking of the fish
No one wants to believe
that the garden is dying
that the heart of the garden has become swollen under the sun
that the mind of the garden is slowly, slowly
draining of green memories
and the garden's feeling
is some abstract thing rotting in the solitude of the garden.

The courtyard of our house is alone
The courtyard of our house
yawns in expectation
of rain from an unknown cloud
The pond of our house is empty
The small, inexperienced stars*
fall from the heights of trees to the earth
And through the pale windows of the fishes' abode
the sound of coughing comes at night
The courtyard of our house is alone.

Father says:
"It's past my time
"It's past my time
"I have carried my load
"and done my work"
And in his room, from dawn to dusk,
he reads either the Shahnameh

---

* A probable reference to the young revolutionaries of Iran who were frequently referred to in the poetry of the time as "stars" or "tulips." Cf. a line from Mohammad Zahari: "Every night a star is killed, /Yet this sad sky with stars is filled."

یا ناسخ التواریخ
پدر به مادر میگوید:
«لعنت به هرچه ماهی و هر چه مرغ
وقتی که من بمیرم دیگر
چه فرق میکند که باغچه باشد
یا باغچه نباشد
برای من حقوق تقاعد کافیست.»

مادر تمام زندگیش
سجاده ایست گسترده
در آستان وحشت دوزخ
مادر همیشه در ته هر چیزی
دنبال جای پای معصیتی میگردد
و فکر میکند که باغچه را کفر یك گیاه
آلوده کرده است.
مادر تمام روز دعا میخواند
مادر گناهکار طبیعیست
و فوت میکند به تمام گل‌ها
و فوت میکند به تمام ماهیها
و فوت میکند به خودش
مادر در انتظارظهور است
و بخششی که نازل خواهد شد.

برادرم به باغچه میگوید قبرستان
برادرم به اغتشاش علف ها میخندد
و از جنازهٔ ماهی ها
که زیر پوست بیمار آب
به ذره‌های فاسد تبدیل میشوند
شماره بر میدارد
برادرم به فلسفه معتاد است
برادرم شفای باغچه را

or Nasekh al-Tawarikh*
Father says to mother:
"Cursed be all the fish and all the birds!
"When I am dead
"what difference will it make
"whether or not there's a garden?
"My pension is enough for me."

Mother – her whole life
is a prayer rug spread
on the threshold of the fear of hell
Always at the bottom of things
she seeks the trace of some transgression
and thinks the garden has been defiled
by the heresy of a sin.
Mother is a natural sinner
She prays all day
and blesses the flowers†
and blesses the fish
and blesses herself
Mother is awaiting a second coming
and the grace that will come down.

My brother calls the garden a graveyard
He laughs at the chaos of the weeds
and counts the corpses of the fish
that turn to putrid particles
beneath the water's sick skin
My brother is addicted to philosophy
He sees the garden's cure

---

* *Shahnameh* is the national epic poem of Iran, written by Ferdowsi (born c. 940) and *Nasekh at-Tawarikh* is a multi-volume nineteenth-century history composed by Lesan al-Molk Sepehr, a court historian.

† The literal translation of "blesses" in this and the following two lines is "blows on," referring to a practice of reciting a prayer and then blowing it upon the person or thing you wish to protect.

در انهدام باغچه میداند.
او مست میکند
و مشت میزند به در و دیوار
و سعی میکند که بگوید
بسیار دردمند و خسته و مأیوس است
او نا امیدیش را هم
مثل شناسنامه و تقویم و دستمال و فندك و خودکارش
همراه خود به کوچه و بازار میبرد
و نا امیدیش
آنقدر کوچك است که هر شب
در ازدحام میکده گم میشود.

و خواهرم که دوست گل‌ها بود
و حرف‌های سادهٔ قلبش را
وقتی که مادر او را میزد
به جمع مهربان و ساکت آنها میبرد
و گاه‌گاه خانوادهٔ ماهیها را
به آفتاب و شیرینی مهمان میکرد ...
او خانه‌اش در آنسوی شهر است
او در میان خانهٔ مصنوعیش
با ماهیان قرمز مصنوعیش
و در پناه عشق همسر مصنوعیش
و زیر شاخه‌های درختان سیب مصنوعی
آوازهای مصنوعی میخواند
و بچه های طبیعی میسازد
او
هر وقت که به دیدن ما میآید
و گوشه های دامنش از فقر باغچه آلوده میشود
حمام ادکلن میگیرد
او
هر وقت که به دیدن ما میآید
آبستن است

to lie in its destruction
He gets drunk,
pounds his fist on wall and door,
and tries to say he is weary,
filled with pain and despair
He carries his disappointment with him
to the streets and to the bazaar
like his ID card, his appointment book,
like his lighter, his hankerchief or his pen
And his disappointment is so small
that every night it is lost
amidst the tavern throng.

And my sister who was a friend to flowers
and would cry, when mother used to beat her,
the simple words of her inner heart
to their kind and quiet gathering,
and would sometimes invite the families of fish
to the party of sunshine and sweets...
Her house is on the other side of town
And inside her artificial house
with her artificial goldfish
in the shelter of the love of her artificial husband
beneath the branches of her artificial apple trees
she sings her artificial songs
and produces natural babies
She –
whenever she comes to see us and the poverty of the garden defiles
the corners of her hem
she takes a bath of eau de cologne
She
whenever she comes to see us
is pregnant.

حیاط خانهٔ ما تنهاست
حیاط خانهٔ ما تنهاست
تمام روز
از پشت در صدای تکه تکه شدن میآید
و منفجر شدن
همسایه‌های ما همه در خاك باغچه‌هاشان بجای گل
خمپاره و مسلسل میکارند
همسایه‌های ما همه برروی حوض‌های کاشیشان
سرپوش میگذارند
و حوض‌های کاشی
بی آنکه خود بخواهد
انبارهای مخفی باروتند
و بچه‌های کوچهٔ ما کیف‌های مدرسه‌شان را
از بمب‌های کوچك
پر کرده‌اند
حیاط خانهٔ ما گیج است.

من از زمانی
که قلب خود را گم کرده است میترسم
من از تصور بیهودگی اینهمه دست
و از تجسم بیگانگی اینهمه صورت میترسم
من مثل دانش‌آموزی
که درس هندسه‌اش را
دیوانه وار دوست میدارد تنها هستم
و فکر میکنم که باغچه را میشود به بیمارستان برد
من فکر میکنم ...
من فکر میکنم ...
من فکر میکنم ...
و قلب باغچه در زیر آفتاب ورم کرده است
و ذهن باغچه دارد آرام آرام
از خاطرات سبز تهی میشود.

The courtyard of our house is alone
The courtyard of our house is alone
All day long, from behind the door
comes the sound of shattering and explosion
Instead of flowers our neighbors plant
machine guns and mortar in their yards
Our neighbors cover their tiled pools
and the tiled pools have become
hidden caches of gunpowder
without wishing it themselves,
and the children on our street
fill their sachels
with tiny bombs
The courtyard of our house is dazed

I fear the time
that has lost its heart
I fear the thought of the idleness of all these hands
I fear the embodied estrangement of all these faces
I, like a school girl
who loves her geometry lessons madly,
am alone,
and I think that the garden can be taken to the hospital
I think…
I think…
I think…
And the heart of the garden has become swollen under the sun
and the mind of the garden is slowly, slowly
draining of green memories.

کسیکه مثل هیچکس نیست

من خواب دیده‌ام که کسی می آید
من خواب یك ستارهٔ قرمز دیده‌ام
وپلك چشمم هی میپرد
و کفش‌هایم هی جفت میشوند
و کور شوم
اگر دروغ بگویم

من خواب آن ستارهٔ قرمز را
وقتی که خواب نبودم دیده‌ام
کسی می آید
کسی می آید
کسی دیگر
کسی بهتر
کسی که مثل هیچکس نیست، مثل پدر نیست، مثل
انسی نیست، مثل یحیی نیست، مثل مادر نیست
و مثل آنکسیست که باید باشد
و قدش از درخت های خانهٔ معمار هم بلندتر است
و صورتش
از صورت امام زمان هم روشنتر
و از برادر سید جواد هم
که رفته است
و رخت پاسبانی پوشیده است نمیترسد
و از خود خود سید جواد هم که تمام اتاق های منزل ما
مال اوست نمیترسد

Someone Who Is Like No One

I have dreamt that someone is coming
I have dreamt of a red star,
and my eyelids continually flutter
my shoes continually pair off*
may I go blind
if I'm lying

I have dreamt of that red star
even while not sleeping
Someone is coming
Someone is coming
Someone new
Someone better
Someone who is like no one, not like father,
not like Ensi, not like Yahya, not like mother
He is like the one who must be,†
taller than the trees of the architect's house,
his face even brighter
than the Last Imam's‡
He does not even fear the brother of Seyyid Javad
who has gone
and donned the police uniform,
nor does he even fear Seyyid Javad himself
who owns all the rooms of our house§

---

* In traditional Iran, shoes were taken off before entering a house. If the shoes accidentally landed together in a pair when they are tossed off the feet, it is superstitiously considered to portend the arrival of an important guest.

† This line refers to the Shi'ite Muslim belief in the anticipated arrival of the twelfth imam, Mahdi, who disappeared in Iraq first in 872 and again in 939. He is expected to return and fill the world with justice.

‡ Again a reference to Mahdi, the twelfth imam.

§ A landlord who owned a large house in a poor district would typically rent individual rooms to various families rather than rent the house as a whole.

و اسمش آنچنانکه مادر
در اول نماز و در آخر نماز صدایش میکند
یا قاضی القضات است
یا حاجت الحاجات است

و میتواند تمام حرف های سخت کتاب کلاس سوم را
با چشم های بسته بخواند
و میتواند حتی هزار را
بی آنکه کم بیاورد از روی بیست میلیون بر دارد
و میتواند از مغازهٔ سید جواد، هر چقدر که لازم دارد،
جنس نسیه بگیرد
و میتواند کاری کند که لامپ «الله»
که سبز بود: مثل صبح سحر سبز بود.
دو باره روی آسمان مسجد مفتاحیان
روشن شود

آخ. ...
چقدر روشنی خوبست
چقدر روشنی خوبست
و من چقدر دلم میخواهد
که یحیی
یك چارچرخه داشته باشد
و یك چراغ زنبوری
و من چقدر دلم میخواهد
که روی چارچرخهٔ یحیی میان هندوانه ها و خربزه ها
بنشینم
و دور میدان محمدیه بچرخم
آخ. ...

and whose name it is that mother invokes
at the beginning and end of her prayers:
"O judge of all judges"
"O grantor of all wishes"

And he can read all the hard words in the third-grade book
with his eyes closed
and he can even take one thousand away from twenty million
without coming up short*
He can take from Seyyid Javad's store
on credit, whatever he needs
He can do things like re-light the lamp "Allah"
which was green, green like the early dawn
in the sky over the mosque
of Miftahiyan†

Ah....
How wonderful is light!
How wonderful is light!
And how much I'd like
for Yahya to have
a vendor's cart
and a propane lamp!
How much I'd like
for myself to sit
amidst the melons and cucumbers on Yahya's cart
and circle around Mohamadiyah Square‡
Ah....

---

* The ruling class in Iran was often called "the thousand families." Twenty million was at that time the population of Iran. The reference here is thus to eliminating the ruling class without effecting the general population.

† A mosque in Tehran with the customary neon light of "Allah" above the dome.

‡ A square in south Tehran.

چقدر دور میدان چرخیدن خوبست
چقدر روی پشت بام خوابیدن خوبست
چقدر باغ ملی رفتن خوبست
چقدر مزهٔ پپسی خوبست
چقدر سینمای فردین خوبست
و من چقدر از همهٔ چیزهای خوب خوشم می آید
و من چقدر دلم میخواهد
که گیس دختر سید جواد را بکشم

چرا من اینهمه کوچك هستم
که در خیابان‌ها گم میشوم
چرا پدر که اینهمه کوچك نیست
و در خیابان‌ها هم گم نمیشود
کاری نمیکند که آنکسی که بخواب من آمده ست، روز
آمدنش را جلو بیاندازد
و مردم محله کشتارگاه
که خاك باغچه‌هاشان هم خونیست
و آب حوض‌هاشان هم خونیست
و تخت کفش‌هاشان هم خونیست
چرا کاری نمیکنند
چرا کاری نمیکنند

چقدر آفتاب زمستان تنبل است

من پله‌های پشت بام را جارو کرده‌ام
و شیشه‌های پنجره را هم شسته‌ام
چرا پدر فقط باید
در خواب، خواب ببیند

من پله‌های پشت بام را جارو کرده‌ام
و شیشه‌های پنجره را هم شسته‌ام

How wonderful it is to circle round the square!
How wonderful it is to sleep on the roof!
How wonderful to go to the National Park!
How wonderful the taste of Pepsi
and Fardin's cinema!*
How I enjoy all the good things,
and how my heart longs to pull the hair
of Seyyid Javad's daughter!

Why am I so small
that I get lost in the streets?
Why does father, who is not so small,
who does not get lost in the streets,
not do something to hasten the day
of the coming of he who has come to my dreams?
And why do the people near the slaughter house,
the soil of whose gardens is full of blood,
the water of whose ponds is full of blood,
and the soles of whose shoes are full of blood,
not do something,
not do something?

How lazy is the winter sun!

I have swept the stairs to the rooftop
and washed the window panes
Why should father only in sleep,
have dreams?

I have swept the stairs to the rooftop
and washed the window panes

---

* A famous cinema owned by the actor Fardin.

کسی می آید
کسی می آید
کسی که در دلش با ماست، در نفسش با ماست، در
صدایش با ماست
کسی که آمدنش را
نمیشود گرفت
و دستبند زد و به زندان انداخت
کسی که زیر درختهای کهنهٔ یحیی بچه کرده است
و روز به روز
بزرگ میشود، بزرگتر میشود
کسی از باران، از صدای شرشر باران، از میان پچ و پچ گل‌های اطلسی

کسی از آسمان توپخانه در شب آتش بازی می آید
و سفره را میاندازد
و نان را قسمت میکند
و پپسی را قسمت میکند
و باغ ملی را قسمت میکند
و شربت سیاه سرفه را قسمت میکند
و روز اسم نویسی را قسمت میکند
و نمرهٔ مریضخانه را قسمت میکند
و چکمه‌های لاستیکی را قسمت میکند
و سینمای فردین را قسمت میکند
درخت‌های دختر سید جواد را قسمت میکند
و هرچه را که باد کرده باشد قسمت میکند
و سهم ما را هم میدهد
من خواب دیده‌ام ...

Someone is coming
Someone is coming
Someone who is with us in heart, who is with us in breath
Whose voice is with us
Someone whose coming
cannot be stopped,
handcuffed and thrown in jail
Someone who has fathered children beneath Yahya's aged trees,
who day by day
grows bigger, and bigger
Someone coming through the rain, through the sound of pouring
  rain, amidst whispering petunias

Someone is coming from Tupkhaneh's sky* on the night of fireworks
and spreads the cloth
and divides the bread
and divides the Pepsi
and divides the national park,
and divides the medicine for whooping cough
and divides the registration day†
and divides the numbers in the hospital‡
and divides the rubber boots
and divides Fardin's cinema
the trees of Seyyid Javad's daughter are divided
and divides whatever's spoiling and remains unsold.
and gives us our share
I dreamt it…

---

* Tupkhaneh is a famous square in downtown Tehran, and has been the scene of many political events.

† "Registration day" refers to the day on which parents would register their children for school. The upper class would typically get priority in this registration process.

‡ Numbers would be assigned to patients in a hospital, and invariably the wealthy, by paying money, would get priority in service.

تنها صداست که میماند

چرا توقف کنم، چرا؟
پرنده‌ها به جستجوی جانب آبی رفته اند
افق عمودی است
افق عمودی است و حرکت: فواره وار
و در حدود بینش
سیاره‌های نورانی میچرخند
زمین در ارتفاع به تکرار میرسد
و چاههای هوائی
به نقب‌های رابطه تبدیل میشوند
و روز وسعتی است
که در مخیلهٔ تنگ کرم روزنامه نمیگنجد
چرا توقف کنم؟
راه از میان مویرگ‌های حیات میگذرد
کیفیت محیط کشتی زهدان ماه
سلول‌های فاسد را خواهد کشت
و در فضای شیمیائی بعد از طلوع
تنها صداست
صدا که جذب ذره‌های زمان خواهد شد
چرا توقف کنم؟

چه میتواند باشد مرداب
چه میتواند باشد جز جای تخم ریزی حشرات فساد
افکار سردخانه را جنازه‌های باد کرده رقم میزنند.
نامرد، در سیاهی
فقدان مردیش را پنهان کرده است
و سوسك ... آه
وقتی که سوسك سخن میگوید.
چرا توقف کنم؟
همکاری حروف سربی بیهوده‌ست

It Is Only the Voice That Remains

Why should I stop, why?
The birds have gone in search of a blue dimension.
The horizon looks vertical
The horizon looks vertical, and motion spins like a fountain
Within the field of vision of luminous planets.
The earth attains repetition on high,
pockets of air are changed into
interconnecting tunnels,
and the day has a vastness
that cannot be contained
in a bookworm's narrow imagination.
Why should I stop?
The road passes through the capillary veins of life
The fertile quality of atmosphere in the womb of the moon
will kill the corrupt cells,
and in the chemical expanse after sunrise
there is only the voice
the voice that will be absorbed in the atoms of time
Why should I stop?

What can a swamp be?
What can it be, except a place for insects of corruption to lay eggs?
Swollen corpses write down the mortuary's thoughts.
The coward has hidden
his lack of manhood in the dark
and the cockroach… Ah,
when the cockroach talks
why should I stop?
Collaboration with lead letters is futile.

همکاری حروف سربی
اندیشهٔ حقیر را نجات نخواهد داد.

من از سلالهٔ درختانم
تنفس هوای مانده ملولم میکند
پرنده‌ای که مرده بود به من پند داد که پرواز را بخاطر بسپارم
نهایت تمامی نیرو ها پیوستن است، پیوستن
به اصل روشن خورشید
و ریختن به شعور نور
طبیعی است
که آسیاب‌های بادی میپوسند
چرا توقف کنم؟
من خوشه‌های نارس گندم را
به زیر پستان میگیرم
و شیر میدهم

صدا، صدا، تنها صدا
صدای خواهش شفاف آب به جاری شدن
صدای ریزش نور ستاره بر جدار مادگی خاك
صدای انعقاد نطفهٔ معنی
و بسط ذهن مشترك عشق
صدا، صدا، صدا، تنها صداست که میماند
در سر زمین قد کوتاهان
معیار های سنجش
همیشه بر مدار صفر سفر کرده‌اند
چرا توقف کنم؟
من از عناصر چهار گانه اطاعت میکنم
و کار تدوین نظامنامهٔ قلبم
کار حکومت محلی کوران نیست
مرا به زوزهٔ دراز توحش
در عضو جنسی حیوان چکار
مرا به حرکت حقیر کرم در خلاء گوشتی چکار
مرا تبار خونی گل‌ها به زیستن متعهد کرده است
تبار خونی گل‌ها میدانید؟

Collaboration with lead letters
will not save mediocre thoughts.*

I am of the progeny of trees
Breathing stagnant air wearies me
A dead bird offered me advice to bear the flight in mind.
The ultimate end of all forces is connection, connection
with the luminous source of the sun
and flowing into the intelligence of light
It is natural
that windmills will decay
Why should I stop?
I place the unripe ears of wheat
beneath my breast
and give them milk

The voice, the voice, only the voice
the voice of the translucent desire of water to flow
the voice of starlight pouring on the surface of the pistil of the earth
the voice of the conception of the seed of meaning
and the expansion of love's common mind
The voice, the voice, the voice, it is only the voice that remains.
In the land of dwarfs
the standards of measure have always travelled
along the axis of zero
Why should I stop?
I obey the four elements,
and the job of compiling the constitution of my heart
does not belong to the local government of the blind.
What's the long howlings of the wild
in the sexual organs of beasts to me?
What's the lowly movements of the worm in the vacuum
    of the flesh to me?
The kindred blood of the flowers has obliged me to live.
Do you know the kindred blood of the flowers?

* "Lead letters" refers to the printing process. Forugh is referring to the fashion of of the time of printing poetry collections, many of which had no literary value.

دلم گرفته است

دلم گرفته است
دلم گرفته است
به ایوان میروم و انگشتانم را
بر پوست کشیدهٔ شب میکشم

چراغ‌های رابطه تاریکند
چراغ‌های رابطه تاریکند

کسی مرا به آفتاب
معرفی نخواهد کرد
کسی مرا به میهمانی گنجشگ‌ها نخواهد برد
پرواز را بخاطر بسپار
پرنده مردنیست

My Heart Grieves

My heart grieves
My heart grieves
I walk the veranda and draw my fingers
over the taut skin of night

The lamps of connection are dark
The lamps of connection are dark

No one will introduce me
to the sun
No one will take me to the party of the sparrows
Bear the flight in mind
The bird must die

Two poems by Persian Poets, Sohrab Sepehri and Ahmad Shamlu, for Forugh.

Forugh with poet and painter Sohrab Sepehri

دوست

I should be glad of another death – T. S. Eliot

بزرگ بود
واز اهالی امروز بود
و با تمام افق های باز نسبت داشت
و لحن آب و زمین را چه خوب می فهمید.

صداش
بشکل حزن پریشان واقعیت بود.
و پلکهایش
مسیر نبض عناصر را
به ما نشان داد.
و دستهاش
هوای صاف سخاوت را
ورق زد
و مهربانی را
بسمت ما کوچاند.

بشکل خلوت خود بود
و عاشقانه ترین انحنای وقت خودش را
برای آینه تفسیر کرد
و او بشیوه باران پر از طراوت بود.
و او بسبک درخت
میان عافیت نور منتشر می شد.
همیشه کودکی باد را صدا می کرد.
همیشه رشته صحبت را
به چفت آب گره می زد.

Friend

I should be glad of another death – T. S. Eliot

She was great
And of our times.
She had relations with all wide-open horizons
And how wonderfully she understood the sense of earth and water!

Her voice
Was like the distressful sorrow of reality.
And her eyelids
Showed us
Traces of the pulse of the elements.
And her hands
Turned the pages
Of the pure air of generosity
And caused kindness
To migrate towards us.

She was in the form of her own solitude
And she explained for the mirror
The most passionate twist of her time
Like rain, she was full of tender repetition.
And she, like a tree,
Would spread into the blessings of light.
She always called the childhood of the wind,
And knotted the conversation
Into the trellis of the water.

برای ما ، یکشب
سجود سبز محبت را
چنان صریح ادا کرد
که ما به عاطفهٔ سطح خاک دست کشیدیم
و مثل لهجهٔ یک سطل آب تازه شدیم.

و بارها دیدیم
که با چقدر سبد
برای چیدن یک خوشهٔ بشارت رفت.

ولی نشد
که روبروی وضوح کبوتران بنشیند
ورفت تا لب هیچ
و پشت حوصلهٔ نورها دراز کشید
و هیچ فکر نکرد
که ما میان پریشانی تلفظ درها
برای خوردن یک سیب
چقدر تنها ماندیم.

For us, one night
She so vividly explained
The green prostration of love
That we touched the sentiments of the face of the earth
And we became fresh like the accent of a bucket full of water.

And so many times we saw
With how many baskets
She would go to pick just one cluster of tidings.

But it was not to be
That she sit before the clarity of the pigeons
And so she went to the edge of nothingness
And lay down behind the patience of the lights
And gave no thought
That we, amongst the confusion of the articulating doors,
For the eating of one apple,
How alone we have remained.

مرثیه

برای فروغ فرخزاد

به جست و جوی تو
بر درگاهِ کوه می گریم،
در آستانه دریا و علف.

به جست و جوی تو
در معبر بادها می گریم
در چار راه فصول،
در چار چوب شکستهٔ پنجره ای
که آسمان ابر آلوده را
قابی کهنه می گیرد.

به انتظار تصویر تو
این دفتر خالی
تا چند
تاچند
ورق خواهد خورد؟

جریان باد را پذیرفتن
و عشق را
که خواهر مرگ است.ـ

Elegy

For Forugh Farrkhzad

In search of you
I weep at the mountain shrine
I weep at the threshold of the sea and the grass.

In search of you
I weep in the passageways of the winds
In the crossroads of the seasons,
In the broken frame of a window
That encloses the cloudy sky
In an old frame.

In anticipation of your picture
How long
How long
Will the pages of this empty book
Be turned?

Accepting the passage of wind,
And love
Which is death's sister. –

و جاودانگی
رازش را
با تو در میان نهاد.

پس به هیئت گنجی در آمدی:
بایسته و آز انگیز
گنجی از آن دست
که تملک خاک را و دیاران را
از این سان
دلپذیر کرده است!

نامت سپیده دمی ست که بر پیشانی آسمان می گذرد
متبرک باد نام تو!

و ما همچنان
دوره می کنیم
شب را و روز را
هنوز را .....

And eternity
Shared with you
Its secret.

So you have become like a treasure
Pleasing and alluring
A treasure of such magnitude
That through you belonging to this earth and countries
Has become pleasant!

Your name is a twilight which passes across the brow of the sky
Blessed be your name!

And thus do we still
Review the day and night
And what still remains....

February 18, 1967

Letters, Interviews, and Articles

A Letter from Forugh Farrokhzad to her Father

Dearest Papa,

It has been a long time since I have written to you. That is, I have written but not sent them. At this moment, there are two envelopes on my desk on which I have written your address, but I have always thought that I should change my letters and that is why they are still on my desk. I don't know what can I write to you. I am well. As always, the more ascetic [dervish] one becomes, the easier life is. Now I have accustomed myself not to expect too much of life. I always tell myself, the way it is, it's good enough. There are many people who are not as fortunate as I am and in this way I do less thinking and more living. Amir is also well. We see each other a lot, and as always, our conversations are about Tehran, the kids, mother, and papa. And this is the only subject that we can talk about for countless days and never tire of it. When we are together, we realize how much we love maman and baba and these kids. How much we always want to have them in our lives and feel their love. I planned to return to Iran at the beginning of the summer, but Amir doesn't agree and thinks I should stay here with him and return with him. I haven't thought it out yet, I miss Kami. But on the other hand, I feel that I am not strong yet emotionally. I am not strong and normal yet. If I return there, that hellish life will being again and I am afraid I won't be able to bear some of the things involved.

You had asked about my work and studies. You know what my goal is in life. It might be a little stupid, but it is only in this that I feel satisfaction and happiness. I want to be a great poet and I love poetry. I have never had any other purpose but this. That is, since I've known myself I've felt that I love poetry. Whatever I do, I do it to expand my intellectual horizons. I never study for getting a diploma or a degree, but rather, my intention is that by expanding the range of my knowledge, I can pursue what I love, which is writing poetry, and to succeed. In the seven months that I lived in Italy, I learned Italian well. I translated two books of poetry from Italian, and now, with Amir's help, I am occupied with translating a book from German. I have also translated one and sent it to Tehran to be published, which, of course, will generate some income. In the last ten month living in Europe I have also written a book of poetry that I intend to publish. Poetry is my God. Meaning that I love poetry to this extent. My days and nights are spent in this thought that should write a new, a beautiful poem—not yet written by anyone. The day that I am alone and have not thought about poetry is considered among my wasted days. Perhaps outwardly poetry can not make me happy, but I have a different meaning for happiness. For me happiness is not good food, clothes or a good life. I am happy when my soul is content and poetry satisfies my soul, whereas if I have all these good things that people kill themselves for and am deprived of writing poetry, I will kill myself. You forget about me, let me be unlucky and always wandering in the eyes of others, but by God, and by the life of my child, I love you dearly. When I think about you, my eyes fill with tears. Sometimes I wonder why God has created me in this way and has put this devil of poetry inside me so that I cannot make you happy and content. But it is not my fault I cannot tolerate an ordinary life like those of millions of people. I don't want to marry. I want to succeed in life and to be an outstanding woman in the society. I don't think you disagree with this.

Write to me , because I love your letters. I want to buy and send something good for you, but I don't know what you like? I have saved some money and want for the first time to buy a gift for my own daddy. But you have to tell me what you like.

Kisses

Forugh

...I feel that I've lost my life, and I know less than I should know at the age of twenty-seven. Perhaps the reason is that I have never had a clear life. That ridiculous love and marriage at sixteen have shaken the foundations of my future life.

I have never had a guide in life. No one has educated me intellectually and spiritually. Whatever I have, I have from myself, and whatever I don't have are those things which I could have had, but which I was barred from attaining by lack of self-understanding, by going astray, and by the impasses of life. I want to begin.

My wrong-doings are not for the sake of wrong-doing. They are due to a strong feeling against futile acts of goodness.

* * * * *

...I feel a stupefying pressure under my skin.... I want to pierce everything and penetrate as far down as possible. I want to reach the depths of the earth. My love is there, in the place where seeds grow green and roots reach one another, and creation perpetuates itself amidst decay. It's as if my body were a temporary and transient form of it. I want to reach its source. I want to hang my heart like a ripened fruit on all the branches of the trees.

* * * * *

...I have always tried to be like a closed door, so that no one would see and get to know my frightful inner life.... I have tried to be a human being, and at the same time be a living presence within myself.... We can trample a certain feeling underfoot, but we cannot deny having it at all.

* * * * *

...I don't know what attainment is, but there is, without doubt, a goal toward which my entire existence flows. If only I could die and come to life again, and see that the world has taken on a new form. A world (which) is not so cruel, and (where) people have forgotten their usual stinginess… and no one has drawn walls around their house.

Accustoming oneself to absurd habits of life and submitting to boundaries and walls are all against nature.

* * * * *

…Is it not ridiculous that a person's happiness should consist of carving his own name on the trunk of a tree? Is this not highly egoistic, and are not those people nobler and finer who let themselves rot without remaining in a single hair, not even a single strand of hair?

…I am glad that my hair is greying and that there are lines on my forehead and two deep wrinkles have settled in my skin over my eyebrows. I'm glad that I am no longer fanciful and full of dreams. I am now almost thirty-two years old. Although being thirty-two means that thirty-two years of my portion of life have passed and come to an end, yet I have found myself in return.

* * * * *

…I was returning home (from the festival)… like orphaned children, I was thinking the whole time of my sunflowers. How much have they grown? Write to me. When they have flowered, write to me…. From here where I am lying on the bed, you can see the sea. There are boats on the water, and it's not clear where the sea ends. If I could be a part of this infinity, then I could be wherever I wanted to be…. I want to die like this, or to go on like this. There always emerges from the earth a power that attracts me. Ascending or advancing are not important to me. I only want to descend, along with all the things I love, to dissolve into one changeless whole. It seems to me that this is the only avenue of escape from annihilation, mutability, perdition, nothingness and nullification.

* * * * *

...Until you attain a freedom of self and separation and release from all the imprisoning selves of others, you will not attain anything. Until you put yourself wholly, completely and totally in the hands of that power which derives its life from the death and non-being of man, you will not succeed in creating your own life... Art is the strongest of (all) loves, and it allows man complete access to its existence when man submits himself to it with all his heart.

* * * * *

...I love our Tehran, come what may. I love it, and it is only there that my existence finds a reason for living. I love that scorching sun, those oppressive sunsets, those dusty streets, and those unfortunate, ill-starred, lowborn, depraved people.

* * * * *

...I wish I could write poetry like Hafez, and possess, like him, a sensitivity that would create a connection with all the genuine moments contained in all the lives of future generations.

A Letter from Forugh Farrokhzad to Ahmad Reza Ahmadi*

...I am very pleased that you have gone somewhere where there is no trace of this phony intellectual life of Tehran. For you who have plenty of intelligence and good taste, and likewise plenty of innocence and purity as well as a pure and impressionable mind, a period of life independent and removed from these shallow and artificial trends can be the best background and aide for your development.

Don't try to write too much poetry. Don't be deceived by excitement and intensity. Let everything subside in your mind. Let everything subside to such a degree that you'd think they had never happened at all. Live so that you'll be saved from monotony. When a man lets himself pass into the current of life, everyday a transformation takes shape in him, and this is what creates man and expands him moment by moment and day by day. When you see that you are repeating one particular idea, put aside paper and pen, just like me – I'm going to put them aside for at least a year. I live and I wait until I can begin again. The fundamental thing is the root which must not be allowed to die. Let the others say, "Did you see how this one† is finished?" If someone says this and you hear it, don't wish to answer him. Just say inside to yourself, "I am not a poetry factory, nor am I looking for a market." I believe that when a man truly reaches the level of creativity, his only duty is to reveal this force apart from any expectations or judgments. After all, what does it matter if the people in the "Riviera" or the "Cafe Naderi"‡[10] feel sympathy for a man at his funeral? A person returns, like a dead man returns to his own funeral, with a fresh and youthful, dazzling presence.

The literary scene is just as it was – a good deal of verbosity and inane talk, and a paltry amount of work.... It sickens me, and as much as I can I am trying to keep myself apart from the radius of these stupid and

* Ahmad Reza Ahmadi, a poet contemporary with Forugh still living today.

† "this or that new talent," refers to poets who would briefly achieve notoriety and then disappear.

‡ Cafe Naderi was a well-known coffee house on Naderi Street in Tehran. The Riviera was another cafe nearby, and both were gathering places for poets and men of letters.

mundane measures and goals. I think of the world, although the hope of becoming worldly is very small, almost zero. But the good thing about it is that it saves a person from the limitations of this confined space and this worm-filled pool, and also, when he is judged and rejected in the despicable artistic circles of this country, he won't be alarmed, but he'll even be taken by laughter. I've written too much.

My dear Ahmad Reza – don't forget the "meter." Listen to me, and never forget it. By God, my wish is that your sensitivity, talent and taste find a flowing channel, a channel that is reliable, firm and stable. Your words deserve to be remembered. I believe that you have not yet found your own form, and this course you are pursuing is not the right way. This thing that you have chosen is not called freedom. It is a kind of simplification and ease. It is just as though someone comes along and tramples all moral laws underfoot, and says "I am tired of all these words" and lives merely according to his whim. In the case of destruction, if its result is not some kind of new construction, then the action in itself is not commendable.

As much as you can, look and live and understand the rhythm of this life. If you even look at the leaves of trees, you will see that they flutter in the breeze with a distinct rhythm. The wings of birds are like this, too. When they want to ascend, they flap their wings together swiftly, but when they reach their altitude, they fly in one straight line. The flowing of water is the same. Have you ever looked at a current of water, at the ripples and swirls? When you throw a stone into a pool, have you seen how the circles dissolve into one another and expand with a distinct, visible form and order? Have you ever noticed the rings in the stump of a tree, with what harmony and calculated form they are arranged alongside each other? If these rings wanted to wend their own way (and grow) without prescribed order, then the trunk of the tree would no longer be a unified mass. In all parts of nature this order exists, this accountability and limitation exists. If you are more attentive, you will see what I am saying. Everything which comes into existence and lives follows a line of distinct forms and arrangements and grows within them. Poetry is also like this, and if you say it is not, and if others say it is not, then they are in my opinion mistaken. If you do not harness force within a form, you have not utilized that force, you have wasted it. It's a shame for your sensitivity to come to naught and for your beautiful and lively words to not find their artistic form. One day you will understand that I was right. I have written too much. I hope I have not wearied you. Write to me, I'll be glad. Regard me as your sister. Though I am late in writing, I write much in exchange and thereby make up for it.

Ahmad Reza Ahmadi (b. 1940) is a well-known Persian poet who was a close friend of Forugh. He has published numerous collections of poetry and has written about Forugh.

An Interview with Iraj Gorgin of Radio Iran – 1964

Interviewer: About your life – (could you give) a description?

Forugh: Talking about it is in my opinion really very futile and boring. Well, it's a fact that everyone who is born has a date of birth, is related to the people of some city or village, is educated in a school, and a number of very common and ordinary events will have occurred in his or her life, which ultimately happen to everyone, like falling into a pond in childhood, or like cheating in school, falling in love in youth, getting married, and these sorts of things. But if the aim of this question is an explanation of things that have to do with a person's work, which in my case is poetry, then I've got to say that the right time (to discuss it) has not yet come; for I have only recently begun the work of seriously writing poetry.

Interviewer: What features should the poetry of today possess? What are the weak and positive points, of the poetry today?

Forugh: I'm very grateful to you for saying the "poetry of today" and not "the new poetry," because the fact is that poetry does not have "new" and "old." What separates the poetry of today from the poetry of yesterday and gives it a new form is the same separation that purportedly exists between the material and spiritual forms of life of today and yesterday.

I think that creative work is a kind of expression and reconstruction of life, and life is something, which has a changeable nature. It is a current that is always in a state of changing form, growth and expansion. As a result, this expression, which becomes art, has its own spirit in every age. If it is otherwise, it is not true; it is not art. It is some kind of fraud.

Today everything has changed. Our world has no relation to the world of Sa'adi* and Hafez.† I even think that my world has no relation to the world of my father; the distances are evident. I think a number of new factors have entered our lives which are creating the intellectual and spiritual milieu of our lifetime. I think that the manner of approach for someone today has completely changed in relation to someone who lived twenty years ago – an approach he has due to different concepts, for example, religion, morality, love, honor, bravery, heroism. Actually, because the surroundings of our lives have changed – in my opinion, all of these concepts are born of the surrounding conditions, (and so) these concepts have changed. I'll give a simple example. We talk about love and the character of Majnun who was, well, the symbol of constancy and steadfastness in love. But in my opinion, since I am a person who is leading a different sort of life, his personage is for me completely ridiculous. When the science of psychology comes along and shatters his (image) for me, it takes (him) apart and analyzes and shows me that he was not a lover, but a sick man – he was a man who constantly wanted to inflict harm upon himself. This is when, well, he completely changes. Just think of him when the Laylis of our time get in and drive race cars at a speed of eighty miles an hour with the police always giving them tickets. Such Majnuns are of no use to these Laylis. But nevertheless, look at our literature. The likes of these Majnuns are still there – though of course we don't call these things "literature," but rather "a (kind of) literature" which is still taken seriously by a number of people – (these Majnuns) are still sitting beneath the same willow trees and are pouring out the sorrow of their hearts to the deer and the crows.

At any rate, "the poetry of today" must be a poetry that embraces the characteristics of our time. At the same time the composer of this poetry must be someone who has attained a certain degree of experience and awareness

* Sa'adi (1185-1292) the great humanist and didactic poet of Iran.

† Hafez (d. 1414) is considered the greatest lyric poet of Iran.

to give the content of his poetry a value that can place it among the (more significant literary) works presented in the world.

Interviewer: What about the weaknesses and strengths of the poetry of today?

Forugh: First let's begin with the weak aspects of our poetry. I think something that exists under the name of the "poetry of today" – and we try to follow this kind of poetry – it is in any event better than the other kinds of things that exist and are still called "poetry," though they have no connection at all to our (present) milieu. But this same poetry (of today) – well, at any rate, since it is a living thing, because it is a living thing, it also contains a certain amount of defects and shortcomings. I think the biggest defect – I don't mean to say just in poetry, but in every creative art, and this is why these types of works do not develop and reach a certain level – is the lack of a (receptive) environment. Here (in our society) art is mainly a diversion, whether for the artist or for the reader. Never, really, have I seen a reader of poetry have the curiosity about a poem to look closely and see what value it has from the point of view of form, and in content what weight, what message (it contains). Many people pursue a bunch of ordinary and childish curiosities that have no relation to these works at all. Since there is no (receptive) environment and no (artistic) current exists, people* naturally retreat into themselves and take refuge in themselves. If they don't have sufficient force, they fall away; and if they do, their verse becomes merely abstract and soulless. This is one of the biggest reasons for the stagnation and lack of development of poetry. Another element is the manner of approach of some people who engage in the writing of poetry. Of course, I make exceptions in five or six cases, and I really believe in them and their way of approaching the concept of today's poetry and today's life. We see this similarly in painting. For instance, a

* Artists and poets.

painter in order to personify the life of today, takes refuge in a bunch of cut-off hands and Kufi script* and things of this sort. These are really decorations and have no real relationship to the spirit of a man of today. These are mere pastimes. The same is true in poetry. I have seen the name of *Taftun* bread and this sort of thing brought into poetry, but this is something superficial, an image. The task of art is expression, to express the existence of a man, the experiential world of a man through a number of images that exist in his material and everyday life. These images themselves are tangible, and when (poets) pursue these sorts of things (as an end in themselves), well, poems become most superficial and childish.

As for the strengths – I think that the poetry of our time, that is, the poetry which began during this decade or before, since the founder of this type of poetry was Nima, one of the most successful poets of the age – one of the characteristics of the poetry of our time which really has value is that it has come closer to the essence of poetry. It has emerged from a form of generalities, a form in which every line would contain a meaning, but as a result we could not develop or clarify any form in our poetry, nor could we impart this form to the reader in a way he could relate to one hundred percent. (Poetry is) to abandon this form of generalities and come nearer to life, to mankind, and to human problems – to problems in which lie the roots of art, and from which art derives its life-blood. It has come closer to these problems, and I hope it will come even closer.

In the poetry of today, which we call such because we are living today, the main point is its poeticality – not poems which are full of sighs and moans, full of sorrow, full of stars, full of tents, full of caravans. Of course even these are not a problem if they come with a modern vi-

* In the 1950s, Persian surrealistic art employed certain traditional motifs, such as old scripts and the depiction of cut-off hands, the latter traditionally symbolizing the martyrdom of Imam Hosein's brother Abbas, whose hands were cut off in Karbela before he was killed.

sion. But the problem is that the world of this sort of people is first of all a world entirely without progress and it has no relation to us, and unless it does, the words have no importance. That which is important in poetry is content, not form. Even in the ghazal form, a man of today, a sincere man, a man who has a sensitivity toward life and does not wish to lie to himself and doesn't want to win the prize for poetry, but rather, it is only for the sake of wanting to compose, to create – even in the ghazal form it is possible to bring forth questions, to lay out issues, the very same issues of today, and create a very beautiful poem. The thing that is set forth in a poem is not its form and structure; it is its content, and if the content of a poem is such that I, in my own age, feel I can relate to it, then based on this it is one-hundred percent poetry.

* * * * *

Interviewer: Although there is no difference between a poet and a poetess, I think that one of the special features of your poetry is its femininity. What is your opinion?

Forugh: If, as you've said, my poetry contains a degree of femininity, it is quite natural, due to my being a woman. Fortunately I am a woman. But if the standard of measurement used is artistic values, then I don't think sex can be propounded (as a determining factor). Discussing this matter is not right in the first place. Naturally because of her physical, emotional and psychological qualities, a woman focuses on problems that are perhaps not apt to be scrutinized by a man, and a feminine "vision" relates to problems that differ from those of a man. I think that for those who choose artistic work as a means of expressing their existence, if they try to make their sex a standard for their artistic work, I think they will always remain on this same level, and this is really not good. If I think that because I'm a woman I should talk about my own womanhood all the time, this would indicate a kind of stagnation and lack of growth, not just as a poet but also as a human being. Because the consideration is that a person nurtures the positive aspects of his or her own existence in some way, so he or she can attain a certain level of human values. The essential thing is being human. Being a man or woman is not the issue.

If a poem can bring itself to this level, then it won't be limited to its composer at all; it will be connected to the world of poetry, it will have its own values, and it will have such impact that a very ordinary man can perhaps reach that level. At any rate, when I write poetry I don't pay so much attention to this issue, and if (my femininity) appears, it is quite unconscious. It is inevitable.

Interviewer: Let's turn to Nima. In my opinion, the first and foremost question for us is always this: What kind of relationship did you have to Nima?

Forugh: Nima for me was a beginning. You know, Nima was a poet in whom I saw, for the first time, an intellectual atmosphere and a kind of human perfection, like Hafez. I, as a reader, felt I was dealing with a man, not just a bunch of superficial sentiments and trite, commonplace words – a factor in explaining and analyzing the problems, a vision and sensibility that rose above ordinary conditions and petty needs. His simplicity always astounded me, especially when behind this simplicity I would suddenly recognize all the complexities and dark questions of life, like a star that directs a person's face to the sky. In his simplicity, I discovered my own simplicity.... But the greatest impact Nima left on me was in terms of the language and forms of his poetry. I can't say how and in what way I am or am not under Nima's influence. The details in this case are for others (to decide). But I can say for sure that from the point of view of poetic forms and language, I am making use of what he attained. But on the other hand, that is, (with regard to) having a special intellectual atmosphere and which is in fact the soul of poetry, I can say that I've learned from him how to look – that is, he depicted for me a breadth of vision. I would like to have this breadth. He gave me an (ultimate) limit (to strive for), which is a human limit. I want to reach this limit. The root is the same, only what grows is different, since people are different. Because of my own psychological qualities and characteristics – for instance, my being a woman – I naturally perceive the problems in a different way. I want to have his vision, but while sitting at my own window. And I think that the difference arises from here. I have never been an imitator. In any case, Nima was a certain stage for me in my poetic life. If my poetry has through change – I don't mean "change" – I mean, if it has become something from which one can start anew, then without doubt it stems from that stage and that association. Nima opened my eyes and said, "Look!" But I learned to see myself. And then before Nima was Shamlu. Shamlu was very important.

[The interviewer suggests that Forugh has been influenced by Nima her choice of words that are "rough" and "shocking," and asks whether she has noticed this influence in her poetry.]

Forugh: Me, no. That is, to the extent of my own power of composition , no. If I had reached this place – which isn't even a place – I think that the personal experiences of my own life were the primary factors. I say this truly and sincerely – there has never been a time when I've wished to write a poem like those of Nima – then what would I be? No, Nima was perfect, and I admired his perfection; I admired the humanness that was in his poetry, I wanted to create that human quality in my own world. I am not one of those people who when they see someone's head hit a rock and crack, conclude that one shouldn't go toward the rock. As long as my own head does not break, I won't understand the meaning of stone. I want to say that even after reading Nima, I have written many bad poems. I needed to grow in myself and this growth has taken time and will continue to take time. One cannot grow tall all at once with vitamin pills. Growing tall is an outward thing, and the bones don't just break *open* (their shells and grow). At any rate, at one time I would write poetry sort of instinctively; it would just well up in me. Two or three a day – in the kitchen, behind the sewing machine. In short, I would just write. I was very rebellious. I kept writing in this way. Because I was reading collection after collection of poetry. I was saturated, and since I was saturated, and I had at any rate a bit of talent too, I inevitably had to pour it back somehow. I don't know if these were poems or not. I only know that there were many "I's" in those days, and they were all sincere. And I know that they were also very easy. I was not formed yet. I had not found my own language, my own form and intellectual world. I was in the small and narrow environment we call "family life." Then suddenly I was emptied of all those things. I changed my surroundings; that is, they changed naturally and by themselves. *Divar* (The Wall) and *Osian* (Rebellion) are in fact a kind of despairing struggle between two stages of (my) life. The latter is the gasps of breath before a kind of release. A person reaches the stage of thought. In youth, the emotions have weak roots, though their attraction is greater. If they are not guided by means of thought, or if they are not the result of thinking, they become dry and die out. I looked at the world around me, at the things and the people around me, and at the basic outline of this world. I discovered all this, and when I wanted to express it, I saw that I needed words. New words, which are related to that same world. If I were afraid, I would die. But I was not afraid. I introduced the words. What was it to me if this (or that) word had not yet become poetic? Each has its own life; we would make them poetic. When the words were introduced, it produced a need for changing and renovating the meters. If this need had not arisen naturally, the impact of Nima could not have done anything. He was my guide, but I was my own maker. I always relied upon my own experiences. I had to discover first of all how it was that Nima arrived at that language and form. If I hadn't discovered (that myself), it would have had no use, I would have been an unscrupulous imitator. I had to traverse that road – that is, I had to live. When I say "I had to," this "had to" explains and interprets a sort of natural and instinctive hard-headedness in me. Besides Nima, many (poets) have enchanted me, like Shamlu. From the point of view of my sentiments and poetic taste, he is the closest poet (to me). When I read "A Poem Which Is Life," I became aware that the possibilities of the Persian language were manifold. I discovered this quality in the Persian language, which is possible to speak simply. Even more simply than "A Poem Which Is Life," that is, with the same simplicity in which I am now talking to you. But discovery is not enough. Well, I discovered – then what? Even imitation requires experience. I had to take a natural path toward this language – inside myself, in conformance with my own emotional and intellectual needs. And this language was created in me automatically. It has been formed in others, too. Now this has become less the case. Isn't it so? I think that I proceeded on this basis with a goal. Now my work has reached a point where I buy newsprint paper. It's cheaper.

Interviewer: When you began (writing poetry), did you turn to Western literature?

Forugh: No. I looked at its content. That's natural. But at the meter, no – it is different. The Persian language has its own music, and it is this music that creates and directs the meter of Persian poetry.

Interviewer: After all your efforts and the avenues you've traveled, what possibilities have you attained?

Forugh: You know, I am a simple person; especially when I want to speak, I feel the need for this (simplicity) even more. I have never studied the prosodic meters; I've found them in the poems I've read. Therefore, they were not a "must" for me; they were ways that others had traveled. One of my good fortunes is that I have never immersed myself greatly in the classical literature of our country, nor have I become greatly enraptured with European literature. I am seeking something within my own self and within the world of my own surroundings – in a particular period that has its own characteristics with respect to social and intellectual life and to the rhythm of life. The secret of the matter lies in this, that we perceive these characteristics and seek to introduce them into poetry. For me, words are very important. Every word has its own special mentality. The same with things. I have no concern with the poetic past of words and things. What does it matter to me if up to now no Persian poet has used a word like "explosion" in his poetry? Day and night, wherever I look, I see that things are exploding. When I want to write poetry, I cannot after all betray myself. If the vision is a modern vision, the language will find its own words and the harmony within these words. When the language has been formed and becomes unified and sincere, it brings its own meter with itself and imposes it on the meters currently in vogue. I put the sentence on the paper in the simplest form that is created in my mind, and the meter is like a thread which passes through these words without being seen, but preserves them and doesn't allow them to fall apart. If the word "explosion" does not fit into the meter and, for instance, breaks the verse, well, this irregularity is like a knot in the thread. One can introduce the principle of "knot" into the meter of the poem with other knots and create a new kind of form and harmony out of all these knots. Didn't Nima do this? In my opinion the time has now passed of sacrificing meaning for the sake of paying homage to meter. Meter must exist. I am convinced of this. In Persian poetry, there are meters that have fewer metrical feet and are less rigorous, and that are closer to the rhythm of speech. It is possible to take those and use them. Meters must be created anew, and the thing that creates meter and must direct the meter is, contrary to the past, the language – the feel of the language, the instinctive quality of words, and the music of their natural expression. I cannot explain these things in this instance like a formula, because the question of meter is not a logical and mathematical thing, however much they say it is. For me, it is a feeling. My ear must accept it. When you ask me what possibilities I've attained in the way of language and meter, I can only say sincerity and simplicity. One cannot depict this with geometrical forms. One has to choose the most genuine and palpable words, even if they are not poetic. One must mold the form into the words, not the words into the form. The excessive aspects of meter must be cut off and thrown away. Will it be destroyed? It will. If your feeling and your words flow with each other without interruption, they will compensate for this destruction of the "conventional." It is out of these very ruins that one can create new things. The ear, when its ability to listen is not restricted, discovers these new melodies. I say all this, but ultimately the key remains somewhat hidden. The difficulty lies in the fact that these two questions, that is, meter and language, are not separate from one another – they go together, and the key lies in they themselves...

An Interview with the Critic, Sirus Tahbaz, and the Novelist-Playwright, Gholam-Hossein Sa`edi – Spring, 1964

Interviewer: Why do you write poetry, and what do you look for in poetry?

Forugh: First of all, this "why" does not go properly with poetry. I cannot explain why I write poetry. I think all those who are involved in creative work have as their motive, or at least one of their motives, a sort of need to struggle with and stand in front of destruction. These are individuals who love and understand life more, and likewise death. Creative work is a kind of struggle to maintain existence, or else to perpetuate "self" and negate the meaning of death. Sometimes I think it is right that death is one of the laws of nature, but it is only in the face of this law that man feels humiliated and small. This is one dilemma about which nothing can be done. One cannot even fight to eliminate it. There is no use; it must be. It is good, too. This is a general interpretation, which may also be foolish. But poetry for me is like a friend to whom, when I go, I can freely unburden my heart. It is a companion that completes me, satisfies me without disturbing me. Some people compensate for their shortcomings in life by taking refuge in other people. But nothing is ever compensated. If it was, wouldn't this relationship itself be the greatest poem of the world and of existence? The relationship between two people can never be perfect nor perfecting, especially in this age. But still, some people take refuge in these kinds of things. That is, they create and afterwards mingle with their own creation, so then they no longer have any shortcomings. Poetry for me is like a window that opens automatically whenever I go toward it. I sit there, look out, sing, shout, cry, merge with the image of the trees, and I know that on the other side of the window there is a space and someone hears me, someone who might live two hundred years hence or who lived three hundred years ago. It makes no difference – it is a means of connection with existence, with existence in its broader sense. The good thing about it is that when someone writes poetry, that person can say: "I too exist," or "I too have existed." How can one say, "I too exist" or "I too have existed" except through this form?

I don't look for anything in my poetry. Rather, I find myself anew in my poetry. But in other people's poetry or in poetry in general.... You know, some poems are like open doors which have nothing on either side of them – you'd have to say a waste of paper. And then some poems are like closed doors, which when you open you find that you've been deceived – they were not worth opening. The emptiness of the other side is so terrifying that it cannot be compensated by the fullness of this side. The foundation of the work is that "other side".... So one has to call these types of works trickery, or jugglery, or a very flat joke. But there are some poems that are not doors at all, and they are neither open nor closed. They have no frames. They are roads, short or long, it makes no difference. One walks and walks and returns and does not get tired. If you stop, it is to see something that went unnoticed in previous comings and goings... A person can stay with a poem for years and still find something new. In these poems there is horizon, space, beauty, nature, mankind; and there is a kind of true mingling with all these things, and a kind of conscious and perceptive looking at all these things. I don't know, my example has become quite lengthy. I like this kind of poem, and consider it poetry. I want a poem to take my hand and take me with it. It teaches me to think, to look, to feel and to see, or else it is the result of a perception, a thought, or an instructive vision. I think that creative work should be one with awareness, an awareness connected to life, to existence, to the body, even to this apple that we bite. One cannot live with instinct alone. That is, an artist cannot and must not. A man must find a vision connected to himself and his world; it is this very need that brings a man to thought and to hope.

When thinking begins, then a man can stand more firmly in his place. I am not saying that poetry should be pensive – no, that is foolish. I'm saying that like any other creative art, poetry must be the result of feelings and perceptions, which have been educated and guided by thought. When a poet is a poet, and "poet" is synonymous with "awareness," then do you know in what form his thoughts enter his poetry? In the form of "A bat that comes from behind the window," in the form of "A lark that has died on a rock," or "A tortoise basking in the sun"* – with just this simplicity, unpretentiousness, and beauty.

Interviewer: You said you always look for a thought in poetry. That is, apart from the form and aspects of feeling, you pay special attention to content. Do elegant, bright and merely beautiful poems therefore not satisfy you?

Forugh: Such poems are only elegant, bright and beautiful. But is poetry something that is merely elegant, bright and beautiful? For instance, these poems that are being published nowadays under the title of sketches – I accept them to the extent that they are elegant, bright and beautiful, if they are indeed that.

Interviewer: But as superb poems?

Forugh: If they possess only these qualities we have enumerated, no. Of course poetry may have several different forms. Sometimes a poem is only a poem – what I mean by the word "poem" here is the concept we have of this word, that is, one-hundred percent feeling, not its general sense. For instance, when we look at a tree at sunset and say, "How poetic it is!" – some poems are like this, that is, they are beautiful. They caress you. At any rate, some poems are poetic. Naturally these are poems, but poetry is not limited to this. These poems have their own place. Poetry is something in which the element of elegance and beauty is one of the components. Poetry is the "humanness" that flows in poetry, not just the beauty and elegance of that human being. For instance, these sketches, when I read them, sometimes I like them. But so what? I like them, and then what? Are all the efforts we make merely to please others? No. The response to art cannot be to merely have

* Quotations are from Nima Yushij's poem, "Makh Ula"

been pleased. These types of works are more the production of a mood than creativity.

Interviewer: We see that those who defend this kind of elegant expression cite Chinese and Japanese poetry as examples, although these poems with all their brevity, elegance and beauty (contain) an extraordinarily human element.

Forugh: Chinese and Japanese poetry is not a mere sketch; it is not a sketch at all. It is a higher feeling and thought which is cast into a short and simple sketch. Moreover, if these poems are short and seemingly simple, it is due to the characteristics of the national environment and mentality that brought them into being. You see the same elegance, brevity and conciseness in all the manifestations of their life, even in the movements of the hand and the syllables of the words of their language. Furthermore, these poems are short and elegant in "form," (but) in "meaning" they are certainly not so. In our case it is completely different. I think what has ruined our poetry is this excessive attention to elegance and beauty. Our life is different. It is rough. It is not refined. One must introduce these conditions into poetry. Our poetry, it so happens, requires a great deal of harshness and unpoetical words in order to be vitalized and live anew.

Interviewer: The questions you've discussed negate many of your earlier poems and even some of the first poems of *Another Birth* – those which are purely sentimental and private.

Forugh: I too say these things to some extent for myself. I criticize myself more than others. It is natural that a large number of my poems will be nonsensical. But at the same time it is not possible to write a definitive formula for the content of poetry, that is, to write that all poems must include universal and public issues. The issue is how a man looks at his own personal affairs or at public concerns. This is the "vision" of a poet that either makes the content of his work private and individual, or else gives a public dimension to the private and personal matters. I accept what you say in the case of some of the poems of *Another Birth.*

When I look at some of the poems of *Asir* (Captive) now, I see that they don't even include my own questions any more, though at the same time their roots were not private.

Interviewer: The question is this, that when an artist reaches the stage where he possesses "vision," the matter of "responsibility" arises. For instance, when one encounters some totally personal and commonplace concerns next to some of your valuable poems – those poems (the likes of) which others scarcely dare to express – he feels sorry. He even begins to think that they were only to fill the book…

Forugh: This is true.

Interviewer: When the poet feels "responsible" – as Nima suggests – this concern must appear in his poetic work.

Forugh: You know, I've said before that there are poems which are in harmony with one's beliefs, experiences and poetic taste. One can "believe" in these poems. Yet there are also poems not in harmony with these things – but a person has an "attachment" to them, for lots of undefined reasons. In this book there are three or four poems which I don't accept, but I like them for no apparent reason. Perhaps it would have been better for me not to publish them. But it is as though I could not be free of them until I had published them.

Interviewer: Here there arises the question of being removed from life and expressing abstractions. Some (poets) believe that a vision of and attachment to (ordinary) life will restrict the reach of their poetry, (and that) they should live in the world of abstractions and flirt with life through intellectual means. They consider expansion to lie in this. Documentable poems in your *Another Birth* are in fact manifestoes against this kind of intellectualism. For instance, one can call your "Earthly Verses" basically a "documented" poem.

Such examples are completely the opposite of those totally private and sentimental pictures.

Forugh: *No.* Under the present conditions I do not condone taking refuge in a room behind closed doors and looking introspectively within (oneself). I say that the abstract world of a man must come as the result of his searching, observation and constant contact with his own world. One must look in order to see and be able to choose. When a person finds his own world amidst people and in the depths of life, then he can always have it with him and be inside it while staying in touch with the outside world. When you go out onto the street and return to your room, the things of the street which relate to your personal existence and your personal world remain in your mind. But if you don't go out into the street, if you confine yourself (in your room) and content yourself with merely thinking of the street, it is not certain whether your thoughts will be in harmony with the realities taking place on the street. Perhaps the sun is shining in the street, and you still think it is dark. Perhaps there is peace and you still think there is war. This state is a sort of negative withdrawal. It does not deliver a person, nor is it constructive. At any rate, poetry comes into being from life. Everything beautiful and everything that can grow is the result of life. One should not run away or negate (life). One must go (into life) and experiment – even the ugliest and most painful moments of life. Of course, not like an awestruck child, but with awareness and expectation of every sort of unpleasant encounter. Every artist must have contact with life. Otherwise, how will he be filled[with ideas]?

Interviewer: That is very true. Your "Visit in the Night," for instance – when one reads this poem, many questions are evoked about it, questions concerning the years close to our (own times). It's as if these poems are the words of a depressed generation that did not believe in its own existence – "The urge to weep clouded the broad expanse of her two eyes."

Forugh: I was looking at the faces of people who once made alarming claims, and I was thinking to myself: "Is this person sitting in front of me the same one who, for instance, was sitting (here) seven years ago? If this man sees that man, will he recognize him at all?" Everything had been turned upside down. Even I had been turned upside down. I hated my own despair, and I was astounded. This poem is the result of these observations. After this poem, I was able to straighten myself out a bit. I revised the text of my thoughts and beliefs and drew a red line through some of my attitudes. But the outside world is still in the same form. It is so upside down that I don't want to believe it. I also worked on the language of this poem. In fact, this was my first experiment in employing a conversational language. On the whole, it's come out with simplicity and ease, though I'm still not satisfied with some parts of it.

Interviewer: In "O Bejewelled Land" – although in the view of some scholars it was not "poetic," and so much the better – there is an admirable proximity to your life. You speak about the inner aspect of circumstances, of your own life. Sometimes you let the "essence of poetry" be sacrificed for "sincerity," and you take your revenge...

Forugh: I never think about poetry narrowly. I say that poetry exists in all things, one simply has to find it and to feel it. Look at all these collections we have. See how limited are the themes of our poetry! They either talk of a spirituality so "high" that it cannot be human, or else they are didactic, elegaic, panegyric, or farcical... And the language, too, is a special and conventionalized language. So what can we do? Our world is a different world. We are travelling to the moon – of course, not us, but others. You think that this is only a very "scientific" matter, but no... Come, and now compose a poem about a rocket. Critics will say "No." So then where is the poet himself? It is as if this "self" should only be a handful of romantic and burning sighs and moans, or else be a "self" forever unlucky and grieving – a "self," which if you touch, the only thing it knows to say is "I am suffering." In the poem, "O Bejewelled Land," this "self" is the society – a society which if unable to say what it seriously has to say in loud cries, at least can still speak through jokes and humor. In this poem I was facing a bunch of crude, rotten, and ridiculous problems. Not all poems should exude the smell of perfume; let some be so unpoetic that you could not write them in a letter and send it to the beloved. What's it to me if you say that they will reject this poem and pinch their noses? This poem has its own language and its own form. When I want to talk about a street which is full of the smell of urine, I can't put a list of perfumes in front of me and choose the most fragrant one to describe this smell. This is deceit, which a man first practises on himself and then on others.

[Some parts of this interview have not been translated as they were either about poems not included in this collection, or about contemporary poets, Shamlu, Naderpour, Azad, and others.]

Interviewer: I know that I'm asking a very stupid question, but let me ask why you sometimes see "life" and "mankind" with such ugliness:

In the ceiling's twisted, crooked lines
I beheld my eyes
Dying like a heavy tarantula
In throbbing, in pallor, in foam

or,

My lot is descending an abandoned stair
to find something in decay and exile

or,

You would see these little criminals
*Standing ...**[6]

Forugh: I said before that a poem is usually the result of the perceptions of a moment. In my opinion, not all moments of

* Excerpts are from "Perception," "Another Birth," and "Earthly Verses," respectively.

life can be imbued with praise. These kinds of vision are sometimes more essential and more realistic than hollow praise of life. When one has looked at all sides of an issue and comes to a conclusion completely given to praise, then that is fine. I am not a philosopher; I am human and I am weak. Sometimes I submit to my weaknesses. Unless I do, I cannot find strength.

Concerning the lines that you chose from the poem "Perception," I have already given an explanation. In fact, the name of the poem itself is revealing. The occasion of the poem, which occurs between the two moments of turning off and turning on the light, is a moment of life in darkness. Getting to know the dark, like getting to know the secrets of puberty, is not an ugly vision, but rather something natural. Every living human being encounters this sort of painful despair and pessimism when he looks at existence only in terms of the form of one individual, namely himself. I am really a meaningless and unfortunate thing if I am not a part of life. I am as futile and void as in the poem "Perception."

In the case of the second quote, I can say that the problem lies in the fact that you are trying to find a clear and definite line of thought in my poems. I am not a philosopher and I don't follow a particular philosophy in my poetry. Perhaps one can say that I have a different sort of vision for different sorts of problems. The logic of this vision is a logic of feeling. Even if we wanted to break down and analyze the concepts contained in these three lines that you read with an extremely dry and mathematical logic, we would (only) reach one root and one principle. For me, "decay and exile" are not death, but rather a stage from which one can begin life with a new outlook and a new vision. It is love itself, minus all the additions and extraneous things. It is a greeting, a greeting to everything and everyone without demanding or expecting an answer. The hands which can be a bridge for the message of fragrance, breeze and light grow green in this very exile. If we don't have understanding and expectations of a form derived from love and life, then we don't see the differences between these things. These are all the various reflections of one feeling, one thought, and one vision regarding the subject at hand. Don't ask me to explain my poems; it is an unpleasant task and in fact, it's ridiculous. In my opinion, one should never lean heavily on one line (of a poem). One must take the whole into account. If we judge these phrases (merely) within their own little framework, problems arise. But if we place them in the intellectual context of the (entire) poem, then the matter is solved. When these couple of lines from "Another Birth" are in fact judged with the whole of the poem, their meaning is completely different. This is one of the characteristics of the poetry of our time – it cannot be (interpreted) line by line.

But concerning the lines you quoted from "Earthly Verses," I completely disagree with you. An ugly vision, especially with regard to mankind, certainly does not exist in this poem. Perhaps one can say it is mixed with compassion. In fact, the whole of this poem describes the atmosphere in which men live, not the people themselves – the atmosphere which pulls men toward ugliness, futility, and crime. I had that crime engendering bubble in mind; the people are otherwise innocent. It is for this reason that they stand and listen to the sound of the fountains. The sensitivity for perceiving beauty has not yet died in them; they just don't believe anymore. This expression of "little criminals" means criminals not by choice – innocent and hard luck criminals. One can even see some degree of remorse and compassion in this expression. This is what I wanted to say, no matter what others get (from it).

* * * * *

Interviewer: Ms. Farrokhzad, we are thankful, we are grateful and much obliged for these interesting comments you've made, for the fine poems you've written, and for the even finer poems you will write. We are not poets, and the things we've said, the questions that have come to our minds, have been in anticipation and expectation of a reader of your poetry, or of every other fine and sincere poet of our country.

You see, for us the "poetry of our time" is very much at issue. To be in this age and to feel the age. If we have talked about the form of poetry here, it was due to the fact that we believe the poetry of our time invites its own corresponding form.

"O Bejewelled Land" and "Spring-time Illusions" – which I never want to call "Green Illusion" – and "The Bird"* seem complete because today's thought is expressed in today's form in them. All in all we see two categories of poetry in this book *(Another Birth):* one approximates your earlier works in terms of form and content, and is less valuable than the poems where you have looked at problems more seriously and more comprehensively, with a new language and vision. The title of "Another Birth" should be applied to these poems, to "Visit in the Night," "Earthly Verses," "The Conquest of the Garden," and a few others....

Forugh: I told you that the poems of this volume are the result of four years of life and labor. I have separated the poems of these four years (from my earlier work) and published them – not only the good poems. On the whole these poems have their own natural qualities, their being either good or bad. Their involution or their evolution is natural. I think I should start anew. A person has to reach a degree of familiarity (with oneself), at least in his or her work. I have not learned to write poetry by reading books; otherwise I would be composing *qasidas* now.

I started like this – like a child who gets lost in the woods, I went everywhere and stared at everything, and everything attracted me until finally I came to a spring and I found myself in that spring – myself, which consists of myself and all the experiences of the woods. But the poems of this book are actually my explorations and my steps in reaching this spring.

Poetry for me now is a serious matter. It is a responsibility I feel confronting my own existence. It is a kind of answer that I must give to my own life. I respect poetry in

* "The Bird" refers to the poem, "The Bird Was Only a Bird." In the case of "Spring-time Illusions," the interviewer inadvertently uses his own title, since the usage of "green illusion" is strange in Persian.

the same way that a religious man respects his religion. I do not think that one can rely on talent alone. Writing a good poem is as difficult and requires as much precision, work and toil as a scientific discovery.

I believe in one other thing, too, and that is "being a poet" in every moment of life. Being a poet means being a human being. I know some people whose everyday actions bear no relation to their poetry. That is, they are poets only when they write poetry. Then it's over. They become once more a greedy, gluttonous, cruel, narrow-minded, abject and jealous person. Well, I don't accept what these people say; I give life more importance. And when these gentlemen clench their fists and clamour and cry – that is, in their poems and articles – it disgusts me and I can't believe they are speaking the truth. I say that perhaps they're raising such a fuss merely to earn their bread. Let's move on.

I think a person involved in artistic work must first of all create and perfect himself, then emerge from himself and look at himself as one unit of being and existence, so that he can give all his perceptions, thoughts and feelings the tenor of universality.

Gholam-Hossein Sa`edi (1935-1985) was a prominent playwright and novelist who suffered torture and imprisonment under the Shah and died in self-imposed exile in Paris after the Islamic revolution. At the time of this interview he had published a dozen of his numerous plays and had become a famous playwright. One of his stories ,"Calm in the Presence of Others" somewhat reminds one of the relations between Forugh and her father. The story of conflicts of an old-generation colonel and her two daughters, is more than a mere generation gap, it depicts a society caught in the crosscurrents of ever-changing values and ideas. (See Sa'edi, Dandil: Stories from Iranian Life *ed. Hasan Javadi. Random House 1981).*

Sirus Tahbaz (1939-1998) was a poet and literary critic, who started his career with the magazine Arash *where the best works of Iranian poets and writers appeared. Many of Forugh's poems and interviews appeared in* Arash. *Tahbaz wrote a book on Forugh entitled* A Lonely Woman: on the life and works of Forugh Farrokhzad *(*Zani tanha: dar bareh-ye zindagi va shi'r-e Furugh Farrukhzad, *Tehran: Entesharat-e Zaryab, 1997). This book includes Forugh's travel account to Italy.*

THE CONQUEST OF THE GARDEN
A Significant Instance of the Poetic Development of Forugh Farrokhzad

Ardavan Davaran [1940–2009]

Speaking of her own early verse, Forugh Farrokhzad said in 1967:

> I used to write poetry kind of instinctively; it would pour out *of me.* Two or three per day, in the kitchen, behind the sewing machine, in any way I would just write. I was quite rebellious. I would keep writing, because I was reading collection after collection. I would become saturated with them, and because I would become saturated and I had a little talent anyway, I had to pour it back somehow...."*

In those days when these poems of "de-saturation" were being poured out by Forugh, my school-mates and I were quite saturated with confusing emotions and natural biological needs of our own. So we were delighted, confused, and excited by the poems of the young poetess – "I have sinned a sin full of pleasure/ In an embrace which was ardent, like fire." The attention given Forugh, by friend and foe alike, was due to her free expression of pleasure about sensual love. For centuries in the great Persian poetic tradition, the expression of a man's love for his fellow man and woman – among them, occasionally, cute camel-drivers – was a repeated, accepted theme. But when Forugh's persona, a woman in her poems, answered back saying "I like it, too!," the entire reading public was provoked. Few said "Why not?"; almost everyone cried foul! But this at any rate made Forugh's poetry widely read and brought about much discussion.

What was new at this point was the bold expression of emotion and feminine passion. The upholders of the *status quo* had pointed their fingers at Nima Yushij, another modern poet a few years before. But that was not because he had sinned a "sin full of pleasure." His sin had been to break down the symmetric and repetitive pattern of structure in rhythm and rhyme in Persian poetry. Forugh rarely went against that symmetry and that repetitive pattern in her early years. Her sin was not one of violating

* *Daftarha-ye Zamare,* 1971, p.79.

form so much as it was one of violating content. With the exception of two or three poems, all the forty-five poems appearing in her first volume, *Asir*, are written in rhyming couplets. With a few exceptions, they are composed of lines of equal length. The same generalization may be made about the poems in the second and third volumes of Forugh's work. In other words, the most distinguishing feature of modern Persian poetry, that of flexible rhyming and rhythmic patterns within a given poem, is missing for the most part in the first three volumes of her published works. Literal expression coupled with consistency of content result in poems that say the same things in the same way and result in lack of effect. Moreover, in most of these poems the poetic language contains outworn images and devices – the coupling of synonyms and antonyms, the presence of over-used poetic clichés. These poems adhere to the use of similes and a conventional sense of continuity. They lack original symbolic images and metaphorical contexts. There are, to be sure, certain instances of more experimental work in these volumes. Most of these experimental exceptions involve mainly variations in rhyme and meter. The poem "Sleep" in the very first volume, besides taking an exception to the lines of symmetric rhythm and rhyme, also includes a metaphorical structure indicative of a finer technique that is to be developed many many poems later.

It is with Forugh's fourth volume of poetry, *Another Birth*, that her "finer technique" evolves. Forugh says of this volume in an interview with the Persian novelist-playwright, Gholam-Hossein Sa`edi, and the critic-writer, S. Tahbaz:

> Now poetry is a serious problem for me. It is a responsibility... to my own existence. It is one kind of answer that I should offer my own life.... I don't think it is possible to depend on one's talent alone. To compose a good poem is as difficult and requires as much precision, hard work and toil as a scientific discovery....*

A composition as difficult to create as a "scientific discovery" is quite different from the kind of poetry she said she used to write "kind of instinctively," those things that would "pour out" of her. Forugh's phrase, "scientific discovery," and the context in which she uses it seem to echo Paul Valéry's phrase, "brutalite sciéntifiqué" in his *Art Poetique*. Indeed,

* *Arash*, No. 13 (1966) pp. 49-50.

the poems in this volume, as well as the poems written after it reveal, upon close study, that they belong to a category of verse new not only in Forugh's own poetic career but also in the development of Persian poetry. In these poems, words are precisely picked; the total structure is carefully construed, resulting in a unique internal correspondence and coherence. Literal language is replaced by a world of images that evoke the experience in the reader. Through a fine fabric of metaphors, personal experience is universalized and perceived as fresh and exciting.

"The Conquest of the Garden" is a fine example of Forugh's mature poetry. It contains one of her oldest themes – the celebration of love, passionate love, and a disregard for conventional affront. Unlike much of her earlier work, though, it reveals, without sacrificing its joyful spontaneity, a sophisticated selectivity and a structural precision rare in modern Persian poetry.

From the beginning a metaphorical language takes command:

That crow that flew
over our heads
and plunged into the troubled thoughts of a wandering cloud,
whose cry traversed, like a short spear, the expanse of the horizon
*will carry news of us to the town.**

The meaning in these lines stems from the association of crows in folk tales with the spreading of tattle-tales. Thus the crow will carry "news of us" – that is, news of our relationship – to the town. The sound of such a bird, like a short dagger or spear, traverses the horizon. The simile here, one of only three similes used throughout the fifty-line poem that abounds in other forms of imagery, alludes to the potential cutting and wounding quality of such a tattle-tale. People then will know.

But what is there to know?:

Everyone knows
Everyone knows
that you and I saw the garden
from that tiny window, cold and stern

* Translations used, unless otherwise noted, are those of H. Javadi and S. Sallée.

and picked the apple from that frolicking branch
beyond our grasp.

What the lovers have actually done is not described in literal, explicit terms. Rather, it is related with reference to the garden of Eden. Thus through the use of imagery that draws a picture of an innocent, natural setting, Forugh conveys the mood or atmosphere proper to the unspecified act or event that has occurred. She conveys the emotional and spiritual context, the events of the lovers' *inner* world. She continues her "description" using images from a Persian wedding ceremony, where light, water and mirrors are present as symbols of illumination, purity and good luck. Forugh thus sanctifies the union of the lovers:

Everyone is fearful
Everyone is fearful, but you and I
joined the water and mirror and light
and were not afraid.

The lovers did not "use" these objects, but rather "joined" with them, furthering the metaphorical sense of these passages. Forugh indeed takes care to remove any possible implication of an actual, formal wedding ceremony when she goes on to say:

The talk is not of a loose bond between two names
nor of an embrace in a registry's old pages.

Thus it is not a question of feebly joining names or of being linked together in an old book of marriage license records. This relationship is a matter of real emotional and sensual communication, of "the sincerity of our bodies in imposture."*

The use of the word "*tarrari*" – "imposture" or "playfulness" – is an excellent example of employing an old word in a new way, out of its traditionally fixed context. In the past, the word was typically used in connection with the beloved or the beloved's hair in deceiving the lover's heart. With Forugh it has lost much of its negative implication, being revived by its

* A. Davaran's rendition of the line translated in the present volume as "our candid bodies in playfulness."

combination with new words and a new context. The word also provides an alliteration in Persian with the phrase "our bodies" – "*tan-ha-man.*" Thus the word brings to Forugh's poem a trace of old associations, and in several ways enriches the line. It is used somewhat ironically, undercutting the effect of the rest of the line that otherwise may have become too melodramatic, too ideal or dreamy.

Throughout "The Conquest of the Garden," nature imagery celebrates the natural and harmonious quality of the lovers' association. This is particularly evident in the following stanza, where the lovers are shown to have learned their ways from nature's innocent creatures:

> *In that green and rippling forest*
> *we asked one night the wild hares,*
> *in that restless and indifferent sea*
> *we asked the pearl-laden shells,*
> *and on that forlorn, triumphant mountain*
> *we asked the young eagles*
> *what should be done?*

Their love thus has the implicit approval of the wild hares, the pearls, the eagles. When the lovers ask these creatures "what should be done," the reference is most likely to the title of the works of different social philosophers, the most famous of which is Lenin's, quite well-known among the intellectuals of modern Iran. But here the lovers ask the natural creatures and not the philosophers what to do, and in so doing they find their way into "the cold and silent sleep/of the phoenixes."

This line refers in part to *The Conference of the Birds* by Fariduddin Attar, the famous Persian Sufi poet who died early in the thirteenth century. The book relates the odyssey of thirty birds in search of the phoenix, the unique and perfect bird. The birds traverse many valleys or stages in their search, and finally reach the phoenix whose name, in Persian, is Simorgh. Attar makes use of the pun inherent in the name Simorgh to show that this unique bird is no other creature than "*si*" (thirty) – "*morgh*" (birds). The phoenix is the embodiment and equivalent of all and each one of the birds. To find the perfect bird, the birds find themselves. Forugh, however, makes an interesting change in this reference. She has very subtly used the word in the plural – "*simorghan*," or "phoenixes." In doing this she remains faithful to the ultimate meaning of the story. Also, she brings the lovers to the level of perfection which the phoenix traditionally represents. But at the same time she brings the ideal bird down from its singularity and exclusiveness to perhaps a more approachable level. There is a cohesive unity in Forugh's use of the phoenix image, too, in view of the images that precede it. When Forugh catalogues the creatures that had taught the lovers what should be done, she ends the list by mentioning "the young eagles" on "that forlorn, triumphant mountain." The reference here is to the mountain "Qaf" where, according to mythological accounts, Zal, the hero of Persian mythology, was reared and cared for by the phoenix. The interlocking network of images is achieved quite subtly and efficiently.

Having followed the lesson of the natural creatures and having found their way into the world of phoenixes, the lovers discover "truth in the garden/in the shy glance of a nameless flower," and they find "eternity" or "existence" in "one infinite moment/when two suns gazed at one another." Forugh's use of the adjective "shy" or "embarrassed" *(sharmagin)* is quite skillful, telling us perhaps that the unknown flower is blushing and therefore red. At the same time it is ironically implied that the lovers are as embarrassed about their relationship as are the flowers in the garden. The abstract concepts of "truth" *(haqiqat)* and "existence" (*baqa,* also translated as "eternity," "continuity," "remaining") are related to corresponding images in this passage of the poem – "existence" or "eternity" illustrated by the propagation of flowers, and "truth" by the two suns that gaze at each other eye to eye.

In the next stanza, Forugh recapitulates that the love in question is not a matter of fearful whispers in the dark, but of daylight and open windows. And once again we observe that the implicative power of imagery rather than the explicative nature of a literal language serves as Forugh's medium of expression:

The talk is not of a fearful whisper in the dark
The talk is of day and open windows
and fresh air,
of a hearth upon which useless things burn
of a land sown with a different seed
of birth, evolution, and pride

As a result of this large and illuminating perspective, the lovers' hands are able to build a bridge of "fragrance, and breezes, and light" and attain a world that is the opposite of night, of the social atmosphere surrounding the lovers:

The talk is of our loving hands
that over the nights have built a bridge
from the message of fragrance, and breezes, and light.

The shift of mood in the next passage to the vocative imperative is quite effective. The poetic voice thus addresses the reader as well as the lovers, and invites them into the world of the poem:

Come to the meadow
Come to the great meadow
and call me from behind the breath of acacia blossoms
just as the deer calls its mate.

This setting where the deer, the flowers and the lover are mingled on the great, vast grassland is contrasted to the world of curtains that we find in the beginning of the next stanza – curtains that cover and keep out light, and that separate those behind them from the world outside. In the next line, translated "The curtains are filled with a hidden gloom," the use of the Persian word "*boqz*" is quite significant. To translate the line literally (and awkwardly) we would have "the curtains are full of a hidden '*bogz*.'" This word has at least two different sets of meanings and associations. One meaning is associated with "a lump in the throat" ("gloom," "sadness," etc.); the other meaning would be "hostility" ("enmity," etc.). The line, then, relates an awareness of the potential danger of those "tattle-talers" who watch and judge from behind their curtains, setting an ambush, as it were. The line also relates the attitude of the lovers towards these upholders of the social taboos. Their dismissal is done subtly and effectively. What gloom should be theirs in those dark rooms separated with curtains from the vast, open natural world:

The curtains are filled with a hidden sorrow,
and from the heights of their white towers
innocent doves
cast eyes upon the ground.

Thus the poem that had opened with the image of black crows as the upholders of social taboo, ends with the image of white doves sitting high upon their white towers – exposed, innocent, and looking down to earth from a very elevated view. A well-knit web of images, such as the crows, eagles, phoenixes and doves, is thus skillfully created in the metaphorical language of the poem. Many images do in fact reach the level of the symbols – the various birds, the curtains and night as opposed to the windows and day, for instance. Forugh constantly chooses her images precisely to fit the totality of the poem, to enrich its implications and arrest attention.

The formal and structural qualities of the poem manifest themselves in an attitude of freedom and flexibility. The poem does not make use of repetitive and symmetric patterns; it contains no fixed rhyme or metric scheme. The continuity of the poem is primarily associative, as when the first person plural point of view, which appropriately reflects a relationship of genuine communication and love, shifts to the vocative imperative mood. And the rhythm of the poem is based upon the natural linguistic flow, and relies on isochronic effects such as "Everyone knows/Everyone knows" or "The talk is not... /The talk is... /The talk is...." Several assonances, consonances and alliterations are also to be found, used always as they are appropriate to the other considerations of the poem, allowing the form and rhythm of the poem to remain flexible and free.

"The Conquest of the Garden" is only one of the poems in the *Another Birth* volume. Poems such as "Green Illusion," the title poem "Another Birth," and indeed most of the poems in the entire collection lend themselves most rewardingly to close study. And this is unlike most poems in most volumes of what is claimed as modern Persian poetry.

After "The Conquest of the Garden," Forugh became more and more involved in the plight of her fellow human beings, and of her fellow countrymen and women in particular. *Another Birth* contains several poems in this direction – "Earthly Verses" and "O Bejewelled Land," for example. But the greater her involvement with these concerns, the more uneasy she became with such controlled techniques as we find in "The Conquest of the Garden" and some other poems of the volume. She began to believe more and more in a freedom of language that would correspond to the ordinary realities of the "street." As she said in the same interview:

> No, I do not accept taking refuge in a room and looking inward under the present conditions.... If you do not go out on the street, it is not certain that your thinking will be in harmony with the reality that takes place on the street.*

This spirit is in contrast to that of the persona of the poem "Another Birth" who had said "In a room the size of one loneliness/my heart/the size of one love/looks at the simple pretexts of its happiness." The spirit wants out, out of the room of any size and onto the street. The new "'street poetry" needed a new language and a new structural concept. With poems such as "Someone Who Is Like No One" and "It Is Only the Voice that Remains," Forugh paves the way for a new direction in modern Persian poetic tradition - a more prosaic type of verse, a "journalistic' approach, that was freer , more spontaneous, and naked. But beneath it all was none-theless, a solid sense of structure. No matter how much of a "street poet" Forugh might have, she had already done more than her homework. She had mastered the metaphor.

* Op. cit. p. 53.

Notes on "Another Birth"

Hasan Javadi

Forugh in one of her letters writes:

> I feel a stupefying pressure under my skin. I want to pierce everything and penetrate as far down as possible. I want to reach the depths of the earth. My love is there, in the place where seeds grow green and roots reach one another, and creation perpetuates itself amidst decay. It's as if my body were a temporary and transient form of it. I want to reach its source. I want to hang my heart like a ripened fruit on all the branches of the trees.*

The idea of becoming one with nature and subsisting through it is not uncommon in Persian poetry. From the beautifully pantheistic quatrains of Baba Taher (d. 1056), where Divine Beauty is portrayed in all aspects of nature, to the more complex philosophy of the great Sufi, Rumi (1207-1273), this human involvement with nature can be witnessed. The evolution of the soul, for instance, is described by Rumi:

I died as mineral and became a plant,
I died as plant and rose to animal,
I died as animal and I was Man.
Why should I fear? When was I less by dying?
Yet once more I shall die as Man, to soar
With angels blest; but even from angelhood
I must pass on.†

Rumi thus sees the evolution of the soul to proceed along many successive stages, leading ultimately to union with the Divine Beloved.

Forugh too deals with matters of life, death and rebirth, though she takes a somewhat different approach. In her poem, "Another Birth," she combines the idea of growth and rebirth with her own creative urge. In her view, it is through art that the artist faces and struggles with death,

* Amir Isma'ili, *Javedaneh*, Tehran, 1968, p. 13.
† *Mathnavi, III*, 3901: Reynold A. Nicholson, *Rumi, Poet and Mystic*, London: George Allen and Unwin, p. 103.

ultimately finding a form of perpetuation. In one of her interviews she says, "Creative work is a kind of struggle to maintain existence, or else to perpetuate 'self' and negate the meaning of death."* Thus in "Another Birth" Forugh tries to perpetuate her love through her poetry, while at the same time trying to discover the meaning of life through her creativity. A general statement she once made about her verse certainly applies to "Another Birth":

> Poetry for me is like a window that opens automatically whenever I go toward it. I sit there, look out, sing, shout, cry, merge with the image of the trees, and I know that on the other side of the window there is a space and someone hears me, someone who might live two hundred years hence or who lived three hundred years ago. It makes no difference – it is a means of connection with existence, with existence in its broader sense.†

In "Another Birth" Forugh mingles the idea of growth and rebirth with a search for the meaning of life and a nostalgic invocation of childhood's bygone days. The idea of rebirth through creativity is introduced in the first stanza:

All my existence is a dark verse
which repeating you in itself will take you
to the dawn of eternal blossoming and growth.

It is reiterated in the seventh stanza – that is, in the approximate center of the poem – as she plants her ink-stained hands in the garden, and it is again expounded in the final stanzas 10 through 13, with such images as the minstrel fairy "who dies from a single kiss at night/and will be born with a single kiss at dawn." Reflections on the human situation and questions about the meaning of life are taken up earlier in the poem, where Forugh proposes various definitions of life – none particularly satisfying- and where she examines life's transience and inevitable movement toward decay:

This is my lot
My lot is descending an abandoned stair

---

* An interview of Forugh by Sirus Tahbaz and Gholam-Hossein Sa`edi, *Arash*, No. 13, Jan. 1966, p. 49.

† Forugh's interview with M. Azad in *Arash*, June 1964, p. 56.

to find something in decay and exile
My lot is a grief-stricken walk in the garden of memories
and surrendering my soul in the sadness of a voice that says to me:
"I love
your hands"

These reflections are followed by pleasant reminiscences of the past, reminiscences of a time when life seemed vibrant and full, almost as if an antidote to the more depressing vision. The final reiteration of the rebirth theme serves to unite or to rise above these contrasting visions, and thus with a circular movement, Forugh returns to where she began – that is, to the affirmation of the poet's role vis-à-vis death and perpetuity:

The journey of a form on the line of time
and with a form, impregnating the barren line of time,
a form aware of an image
which returns from the party of a mirror.
And it is thus
that someone dies
and someone remains

Interestingly, the theme of death runs side by side that of life throughout the poem, as in stanzas two and three where Forugh wonders if life is a rope with which a man hangs himself, or refers to life as the lighting of a cigarette "in the languid repose between two embraces." When Forugh was attempting to translate this line into English with the help of a friend, Karim Emami, she wanted to find a word for "*hamaghushi*" (embrace or love-making) which would connote the idea of death as well, since she says she also had that connotation in mind.*

Pondering the question of life, Forugh also asks herself if it is the routine walk of a woman on a long street, or a child returning from school, or an absent-minded passer-by who tips his hat absentmindedly to another passer-by. Forugh in this case sees life to be merely a transient period marking a larger cycle, and indeed each of these three images illustrates someone in motion, someone in transit from one place to another, rather

* Karim Emami, "Az Khak be Khak, Az Jahan be Jahan," *Arash*, no. 13, p.122.

than someone stationary or arrived. According to her own comments on the poem: "Our stay in this world is so short that the important thing is the perception (or, the impression) that more lasting elements such as the moon or the night might have on our position here, not vice versa"* – and indeed this comment may shed some light on what Forugh means when she refers to the sensation "which I will mingle with the perception of the moon and the discovery of darkness." To Forugh this life consists mostly of lonely and depressing events; it is short, and Forugh is yearning and searching for something more enduring. And it is through nature and creativity that she hopes to attain this higher stage.

In the above-mentioned English translation of "Another Birth," made jointly by Karim Emami and Forugh, the word *"ayeh"* (verse) was rendered as "chant," with the explanation that "What she meant was something imperishable like the word of God."† Forugh thus regards her life as some dark, magical "chant," which while "repeating" the beloved – or perhaps simply the listener – in itself will take her to "the dawn of eternal blossoming and growth" and graft her to the elements of nature such as "tree and water and fire." The image somewhat parallels that of physical pregnancy and birth, though it is the *"ayeh"* or verse that carries the "child"-that is, the beloved or the listener-in itself and eventually "gives birth." It is thus through poetry for Forugh that perpetuation will take place.

Through such natural imagery Forugh expresses her deep affinity with nature and its cycles. According to an Iranian critic of *Another Birth*, "sincerity flows like water – sincerity toward things and more particularly toward nature. There is no need for reasoning. This sincerity, more than being logical, is tangible."‡ Even when Forugh speaks of her own introduction to poetry, an attachment to nature is obvious. In one of her interviews she says:

> I became acquainted with poetry like a child. A child sees a red spot in the garden. She goes toward it and touches it. She finds it soft and delicate. It is a petal. It is fragrant and there are other petals. It is a rose with a stem, a branch, leading to roots. Becoming curious, the child finds out that there are other flowers, with different colors and scents...."

* Ibid. p.122.

† Ibid. p.121.

‡ Ebrahim Moqqala, "Forughi digar dar Tavaludi digar" (Another Forugh in Another Birth), *Arash*, II No. I, (June, 1963), p. 160.

Examples of nature imagery are indeed numerous in all of Forugh's poetry; one has only to look at the titles for this to become clear – "Red Rose," "On the Earth," "I Will Greet the Sun Once Again," and so on. "Another Birth" is no exception, the very idea of rebirth, as we have seen, being connected in Forugh's mind with natural processes and things. In the first stanza, being taken to "the dawn of eternal blossoming and growth" is parallel not only to the implied process of pregnancy and birth, but also to the following explicit image of being grafted to the elements of "tree and water and fire." In the seventh stanza self perpetuation is again envisaged in natural terms, this time as the process of planting, growth and interaction with other natural creatures:

I plant my hands in the garden
I will grow green, I know, I know, I know
and in the hollows of my ink-stained fingers
swallows will lay eggs.

Thus it is Forugh's very hands, stained perhaps with the ink of her poetic art, that become for her the source of fertility and generation. Birth and rebirth are for Forugh both a part of nature's cycles and a part of the more spiritual/intellectual process of creative art.

A few words should perhaps be said about stanza 10, where Forugh departs to some degree from her more accessible nature imagery to speak of her theme in more abstract and philosophical terms. In this stanza the word "form" (*"hajm,"* volume or mass) presents difficulties for translation. Forugh and Emami faced this difficulty and chose the word "form" for "*hajm,*" considering it to be "a noun denoting volume which is neither so precise nor so vague that it cannot be counted."* Their translation of the entire stanza is as follows:

The journey of a form along the line of time
and inseminating the line of time with the form, a form
conscious of an image
returning from a feast in the mirror.†

* Karim Emami, op. cit., p.122.
† Ibid. p.126.

According to Forugh herself in the same article, *"hajm"* here represents the human mind and thought, whereas the "image" indicates the physical and superficial aspects of life. While man is alive, his external life is "a feast in the mirror," and that which is permanent are his thoughts, or *"hajm"* – that is, the thoughts of a powerful mind will occupy a larger volume on the line of time and leave their imprint for generations to come. Moreover, these thoughts which inseminate the "dry line of time" are conscious of the external image, of the superficial and transient aspect of life, and can presumably see this level of life simply for what it is. Stanza 12, where Forugh asserts that "In the shallow stream that flows into a ditch, no fisherman will hunt a pearl," further confirms Forugh's sense of need for the higher type of vision expressed through this image of *"hajm"* and the "line of time"-namely, that no pearls of price, no great attainments of wisdom or of being, will be found in the shallow or superficial aspects of life that are doomed inevitably to decay. Sights must be set higher, and it is insofar as they are or are not that perhaps "someone dies/and someone remains."

The last stanza returns to Forugh's less philosophical and more accessible imagery, and it serves as the summation of Forugh's attitudes and vision of rebirth. The sad little fairy who lives in the ocean and plays her heart on a wood-tipped flute is of course the poetess herself-indeed, she is possibly the very girl "whom one night the wind bore away" (Stanza 8), who now is "sad" instead of "innocent" because she has witnessed and experienced the transient aspects of life described in stanzas two through six which lead to loss and decay. Forugh in her own translation changes the "wood-tipped flute" of the Persian into a "magical flute," saying that she was originally looking for such a word but could not find anything to fit with the line.* The "magical" quality of the stanza is at any rate clear, with the "fairy" who lives in the ocean-that is, in the natural world-yet at the same time lives outside of certain physical laws, dying "from a single kiss at night" and being born "with a single kiss at dawn." Indeed, many things in this stanza contrast with earlier images of the poem – the depth of the ocean, for instance, is in contrast to the shallowness of the stream in stanza 12; the ethereal fairy is in contrast to such harsh realities of life as the man who hangs himself with a rope. Even the intensity of thought in stanzas ten through twelve is relieved in the final stanza by the magical

* Ibid. pp.122-23.

mood and the calm of the flute which plays softly and simply the song of the heart – the final symbol of the poet's art. It should be noted too that the reed or flute has numerous associations in Persian literature. In the "Song of the Reed," Rumi's famous introduction to his *Mathnavi,* the reed symbolizes the human soul that laments and seeks to return to its source. It also represents the reed pen that the Sufi poet uses to describe the pains of separation from the Divine Beloved. Having these connotations in mind, as well as the imagery and movement of her own poem, Forugh aptly makes the "wood-tipped flute" a symbol for her poetic art in its exploration of matters of life and regeneration.

A Timeline of Forugh Farrokhzad's Life

1935	Born on 5 January 1935 in Tehran.	Fourth of seven children of Turan Vaziritabar and Colonel Mohammad Farrokhzad.
1940–1946	Elementary school education in Tehran.	
1946, September	Begins high school at Khosrow Khavar School in Tehran.	According to Forugh, she was writing traditional *ghazals* that she never published. Her favorite poet was Mehdi Hamidi, and she says she never learned traditional Persian prosody.
1949, September	Enters Art School of Kamal al-Molk for learning painting and dress-making.	In painting, Forugh found a permanent, second venue of artistic expression. But poetry was foremost in her mind. She says: "I had no guide to direct my talents. In this period I was full of poetry and write three or four poems every day in the kitchen or behind the sewing machine."
1950, 14 September	Marries Parviz Shapur (b. 1919), a second cousin	Both families were against the marriage. Forugh said: "That ridiculous marriage at the age of sixteen destroyed my future life." that night when I felt the pain and the seed was conceived that night when I became the bride of acacia blossoms that night when Isfahan abounded with the echoes of blue tiles, and that man who was my mate had returned within my seed... Suddenly he called me and I became the bride of acacia blossoms... from "Let us Believe in the Coming of a Cold Season." At this time, writing poetry was a "pastime" for Forugh, who said, "because I was reading collection after collection of poetry, I was saturated, and since I was saturated, and I had at any rate a bit of talent too, I inevitably had to pour it back somehow. I don't know if these were poems or not. I only know that there were many 'I's' in those days, and they were all sincere. And I know that they were also very easy."
1951	Moves to Ahwaz with her husband who had found a job there	
1952, Spring	Publication of her collection *The Captive*	

1952, 19 June	Her only son Kamyar (Kami) is born	After the birth of Kamyar, Forugh became "a real woman" and she blossomed in her womanhood. But intellectually, she said: "I was not formed yet. I had not found my own language, my own form and intellectual world. I was in the small and narrow environment we call 'family life.' Then suddenly I was emptied of all those things. I changed my surroundings; that is, they changed naturally and by themselves."
1953–54	Forugh makes frequent trips to Tehran from Ahwaz	She publishes in progressive periodicals such as *Ferdowsi*. In "Ramideh" Forugh expresses, in perhaps a more general way, the agony of living amidst a world that cannot understand, much less condone, the desires that arise and stir in her inner life. She writes: I flee from all these people who with me To friendship and sincerity pretend But inwardly, replete with paltriness Tie two hundred spangles to my hem. These people, when they hear my poetry, Smile like fragrant flowers to my face, But call me a mad woman of ill fame When sitting in their own secluded place.
1955, 2 January	On the occasion of "Women's Day" she writes a poem "To my Sisters"	In her letters to the editor of *Omid-e Iran* she wrote: "My wish is that Iranian women gain equal rights with men. I am fully aware of the sufferings of my sisters in this country as a result of the injustices of men. I devote half of my art to picture their sufferings. I wish that Iranian men give up their selfishness and allow women to show their talents and art. My wish is to create a suitable atmosphere for the social and artistic activities of Iranian women.
1955, Summer & Fall	Forugh gets divorced and looses custody of Kamyar, which goes to the father.	When Shapur's mother does not allow her to see Kamyar, she is devastated and wonders aimlessly for hours in the streets of Tehran. After publication of her the poem "Sin" and her other poems, many poets and writers in Tehran befriend her. But her father, who said, "Forugh has brought shame to our family," was against her. Later on, he sends her out of the house with a suitcase. Forugh had nowhere to go. Years later Forugh wrote to her father, "My great grief is that you never understood me, and never tried to do so. Perhaps you still think that I am a fool-headed woman with stupid thoughts, her brains brimming with silly romances. I wished I could be such a woman and be happy with a mediocre husband."

1955, Fall and Winter	Forugh has a nervous break down and spends one month in a psychiatric clinic.	After this shock she found an assertive, even a combative voice. It was not her lack of reservation in talking about sexuality that brought Forugh to the forefront of the literary scene, but her genuine female voice, unprecedented amongst the poetesses of Iran, that gained her notoriety in the stifling atmosphere of the Iran of the 1953 coup d'etat. It was at this time that she came to know the poets Sohrab Sepehri, and Mehdi Akhavan-Saless, who in his poem "Winter" had described the foreboding political scene where no one would bring out his hand and greet you even though you extended your hand toward them.
1956, Spring–Summer	Forugh goes to Italy in late spring and her collection *Divar* (The Wall) is published in early summer.	About going to Italy she says, "I wanted to be free from society's chains on my hands and feet. I was tired and distressed. I wanted to be a 'woman' that is a 'human being.'" After seven months in Italy she goes to stay with her elder brother in Munich, and with whom she translates a collection of some German poets *(My death will come one Day)*. "I needed to grow in myself and this growth has taken time and will continue to take time. One cannot grow tall all at once by taking vitamins. Day and night I think of writing a new poem, a poem the likes of which has not been written yet. A day that I am not alone and don't think about poetry I consider a wasted day."
1956, mid-summer	She returns to Tehran and has nowhere to live and no income.	Forugh writes an account of her travels in Europe in *Ferdowsi,* which is left unfinished after eight articles. She writes two short stories "Nightmare" and "Indifferent" for the same magazine. Her private life still raises eyebrows. In "A Poem for you" she writes: I was the one branded with shame Who laughed at vain taunts and cried: 'Let me be the voice of my own existence!' But alas, a 'woman' was I.
1958	Her collection *Osian* (Rebellion) is published.	Forugh says about that period in her life: "Then suddenly I was emptied of all those things [family life]. I changed my surroundings; that is, they changed naturally and by themselves. *Divar* (The Wall) and *Osian* (Rebellion) are in fact a kind of despairing struggle between two stages of (my) life. The latter is the gasps of breath before a kind of release. A person reaches that stage of thought.
1958, October	Forugh becomes friends with Ebrahim Golestan and starts working in his film studio.	Their life-long love begins.

1959, Summer	Forugh and Samad Kamalipur are sent by Golestan Studio to England and Holland.	Returning to Iran after seven months, Forugh starts acting, and producing documentary films with Golestan.
1960, September	Forugh begins to publish some of the poems of her later collection *Another Birth* in *Andisheh va Hunar, Ketabe Hafteh* and *Arash.*	She is involved with Golestan in making a series of six documentaries for the Pars Oil Company. She acts in Bernard Shaw's "Mrs. Warren's Profession" and then in a film, "The Sea," directed by Golestan, which was based on a story, "Why the Sea Became Stormy?" by the writer Sadeq Chubak.
1962, Summer	Forugh goes to Tabriz to make a documentary film.	She films the lives of lepers in the lepers colony of "Baba Baghi."
1962, Fall	Forugh returns to Tabriz with her film crew to finish her documentary about the lepers, "The House is Black"	In the leper colony she adopts an orphan boy, Hosein, who was the same age as Kami. She writes: "Grief and sadness would not leave me alone. They would kill me. When Hosein came it became better. In the face of this boy I see Kami. When I caress his hair, I would not think that he is Hosein or Kami…There is no difference. I only think that this is my son."
1963, 19 February	Showing of "The House is Dark" at the Film Center of Tehran creates a sensation, and it gets good reviews.	
1963, Spring	Forugh acts in films and plays.	She acts in the last parts of the film "Mirror and the Brick," as well as in Luigi Pirandello's play, "Six Characters in Search of an Author" at the Iran-Italy Cultural Center.
1963, Spring	Her poem "O Bejewelled Land" is published in *Arash.* Soon after her collection *Another Birth* is published. It is dedicated to Ebrahim Golestan.	She said: "The poems of this volume are the result of four years of life and labor. I have separated the poems of these four years (from my earlier work) and published them – not only the good poems. On the whole these poems have their own natural qualities, their being either good or bad. Their involution or their evolution is natural. I think I should start anew. A person has to reach a degree of familiarity (with oneself), at least in his or her work. I have not learned to write poetry by reading books; otherwise I would be composing *qasidas* (a traditional poetic style) now.

1963, Winter	Short trip to Germany to attend the Oberhausen Festival where "The House is Dark" had won the prize for best documentary.	She says in an interview: "If, as you've said, my poetry contains a degree of femininity, it is quite natural, due to my being a woman. Fortunately I am a woman. But if the standard of measurement used is artistic values, then I don't think sex can be propounded (as a determining factor)." In an interview she says: "Cinema for me is a means of expression. Although I have written poetry all my life, there is no reason that it should be my only means of expression. I like films and in any way that I can I will make use of it. If I could not write poetry I would act in the theater. If I could not do that, I would make films. Continuing this, of course, depends on if I have something to say. "
1963, Spring	UNESCO produced a thirty minutes movie about Forugh.	Bernardo Bertolucci came to Iran to interview her and decided to produce a fifteen-minute movie about the poetess's life.
1964, June		Forugh buys a small house on an installment plan near Golestan's studio. It becomes a gathering place for young artists and poets: Sa`edi, Tahbaz, M. Azad, Bijan Jalai to name a few. Numerous interviews are done with her and published.
1964, Summer	Selected Poems of Forugh (her own selection) is published.	She says at this time: "Poetry for me is like a window that opens automatically whenever I go toward it. I sit there, look out, sing, shout, cry, merge with the image of the trees, and I know that on the other side of the window there is a space and someone hears me, someone who might live two hundred years hence or who lived three hundred years ago." According to her sister Puran, Forugh tried to commit suicide four times. Puran writes, "Every so often she (Forugh) would get depressed and would close the door of her room and cry. Her old maid would call my mother to say that she has again closed the door of her room. She would do all her crazy things of her life in these days." Forugh herself said, "I have always tried to be like a closed door, so that no one would see and get to know my frightful inner life."
1965, Spring	Trip to Italy and France.	
1965, Fall	Bernardo Bertolucci comes to Iran and visits Forugh and Golestan.	He gets copies of their films for his own archive.

1965 November	Her poem "Let Us Believe in the Coming of a Cold Season" is published in *Arash.*	"I feel a stupefying pressure under my skin.... I want to pierce everything and penetrate as far down as possible. I want to reach the depths of the earth. My love is there, in the place where seeds grow green and roots reach one another, and creation perpetuates itself amidst decay. It's as if my body were a temporary and transient form of it. I want to reach its source. I want to hang my heart like a ripened fruit on all the branches of the trees."
1966 Spring	A four-month trip to Italy to participate in the film festival at Pesaro.	According to Puran, a gypsy girl had read Forugh's palm and told her that she would have a bloody accident. Forugh had mentioned this several times. Forugh helps Hamid Samandarian translate Brecht's *The Caucasian Chalk Circle* for which she versifies its poems.
1966 Summer	"Someone Comes Who Is Not like Any Other" is published in *Arash.*	Forugh says, "...I am glad that my hair is graying and that there are lines on my forehead and two deep wrinkles have settled in my skin over my eyebrows. I'm glad that I am no longer fanciful and full of dreams. I am now almost thirty-two years old. Although being thirty-two means that thirty-two years of my portion of life have passed and come to an end, yet I have found myself in return."
1967, 4 February		The poet Yadollah Royai writes: "I had given a party and there were many writers, poets and artists there. Forugh was there too and wrote a poem on a piece of paper. While saying goodbye she gave me the paper. She had written on the margin: "Remember the flight. The bird will die." Then she said goodbye. The poem was: My heart grieves My hear grieves I walk the veranda and draw my fingers Over the taut skin of night The lamp of connection is dark The lamp of connection is dark No one will introduce me to the sun No one will take me to the party of the sparrows Remember the flight. The bird will die.

1967, 14 February	Forugh dies in a car accident.	Forugh did not have a good driving record and had been involved in several accidents previously. On that day Forugh had lunch with her parents, and after lunch her father wanted to give her a ride, but she said: "You drive so slowly that one gets restless." Instead, she herself drove the car that had been sent by the studio. With Forugh behind the wheel, at the intersection of Marvdasht and Loqman al-Molk Streets in Darrus, she swerved the jeep to avoid an oncoming vehicle and struck a wall. Thrown from her car, she died of head injuries at the height of her creative powers. She was buried, while snow fell, the Zahir-al Dowleh cemetery in Tehran. She had said: "Sometimes I think it is right that death is one of the laws of nature, but it is only in the face of this law that man feels humiliated and small. This is one dilemma about which nothing can be done. One cannot even fight to eliminate it." In "Meeting at Night" she wrote: I am not sorry, As if my heart is beating beyond those ages Life will repeat my heart And dandelions traveling over the windy lake Will take my message.

The jeep that Forugh was driving after the accident that killed her.

Select Bibliography

In Persian

Arash, no. 13 (Feb. /March, 1967), Some interviews, letters and writings by Forugh: 1-69.

Abedini, Farhad, "Sayri dar Surudeh-ha-ye Forugh." *Negin,* nos. 129/130 (Feb./March, 1977):9-14, 23-28.

Aryanpour, A.J. "Zamineh-ye Ejtema'i-ye She'r-e Farsi," *Payam-e Novin 7, No. 4* (March/April, 1965):1-8, 66-93.

Baraheni, Reza, "Farrokhzad, Bonyangozar-e Mektab-e Mo'annas-e She'r-e Farsi," *Ferdowsi* 20 (1970/71): No. 950:20.

"Salha-ye Ashna'i ba Forugh va She'rash," *Ferdowsi* 24 (1973/74), no. 117:22-25. "Ta'amulati Piramun-e She'r va Nathr," *Negin,* no. 168 (June 1979):13-16, 46-48.

Behbahani, Simin, "Forugh: Aseman-e Por az Pulak," *Iran Express 2, no.* 12 (March 24, 1979): 17.

Dastghayb, 'Abdol-'Ali, "Forugh Farrokhzad," *Payam-e Novin* 10, no. 10 (May-August 1974): 8-24.

"She'r-e Forugh," *Negin 2* (1966/67), no. 10:15-17, 98.

Farrokhzad, Forugh, in collaboration with Majid Rowshangar, *Az Nima to Ba'd,* Tehran: Morvarid, 1968.

———. *Bargozideh-ye Ash'ar-e Forugh Farrokhzad,* 3rd ed. Tehran, Ketabha-ye Jibi, 1973.

———. *Divar,* 5th ed. Tehran: Amir Kabir, 1973.

———. *Osian,* 6th ed. Tehran: Amir Kabir, 1973.

———. *Asir,* 8th ed. Tehran: Amir Kabir, 1973.

———. *Tavallodi Digar,* 3rd ed, Tehran: Morvarid, 1968.

———. *Iman Biyavarim Be Aghaz-e Fasl-e Sard,* 1st ed. Tehran: Morvarid, 1974.

———. *Avvalin tapish-ha-yi 'ashiqanah-yi qalbam: namah-ha-yi Furugh Farrukhzod bih hamsarash Parviz Shapur ; bih kushish-i Kamyar Shapur va 'Umran Salahi.* Tehran, Morvarid, 2002.

———. *Harfha'i ba Forugh Farrokhzad.* Vincenne, France, Khavaran, 1368 [1989]

———. *Marg-i man ruzi : majmu'ah'i az nemuneh-ha-yi ash'ar-i shu'ara-yi Alman dar nimah-yi avval-i qarn-i bistum* / translated by Furugh Farrukhzad, Mas'ud Farrukhzad. Tehran, 1377 [1998]

———. Khanah siyah ast [videorecording](The House is Black/La Maison Est Noire) In film bih sifarish-i Jam'iyat-i Kumak bih Juzamiyan dar sazman-i Film-i Gulistan sakhtah; tahayah kunandah, Ibrahim Gulistan ; payvand va kar gardani, Furugh Farrukhzad. Laguna Niguel, California, Iranian Movies, 2003

Haydari Ghulam, Furugh Farrukhzad va sinima. Tehran, Nashr-i 'Ilm, 1377 [1998]

Hoquqi, Mohammad, *She're-Nov az Aghaz to Emruz.* Tehran: Ketabha-ye Jibi, 1974.

———. "Tavallodi Digar, Naqus-e Hoshdar," *Arash,* no. 7 (June/July, 1964):146-152.

———. *Shi'rha-ye Forugh Farrukhzad az aghaz ta imruz / shi'rha-ye barguzidah, tafsir va tahli-i muvaffaqtarin shi'rha,* Tehran, Agah, 1372 [1993].

Kalbasi, Mohammad, "Tanha Seda'st keh Mimanad," *Payam-e Novin 8, no.* 9 (March/ April, 1967):12-18.

Kamyar, 'Abidi, *Tanhatar az yak barg : zindagi va shi'r-i Furugh Farrukhzad.* Tehran, Jami, 1377 [1998]

Mirsadeqi, Maymanat, *Bibliography of Persian New Poetry,* Tehran: Anjoman-e Ketab, 1976.

Mokalla, Ebrahim, "Foroughi Digar dar Tavallodi Digar," *Arash,* no. 7 (June/ July, 1964); 153-162.

Nuri 'Ala, Esma'il, *Sovar va Asbab dar She'r-e Emruz-e Iran,* Tehran: Bamdad, 1969.

Amir Esma'ili and Abul-Qasim Sadarat, *Javedaneh Forugh Farrokhzad,* 2nd ed. Tehran: Marjan, 1968.

Nikbakht, Mahmud, *Az gumshudagi ta rahayi,* 1st edition. Isfahan: Mash'al, 1372 [1993].

Shamisa, Sirus, *Nigahi bih Furugh Farrukhzad / Sirus Shamisa.* Tehran, Morvarid, 1993.

Tahbaz, Sirus, *Zani tanha: dar bareh-ye zindagi va shi'r-e Furugh Farrukhzad,* Tehran: Entesharat-e Zaryab, 1997

In English

Aryanpour, Manouchehr, "The Wind-up Doll," tr. *World Literature Today,* 46 (1968):248-249.

Banani, Amin & Jascha Kessler, *Bride of Acacia: Selected Poems of Forugh Farrokhzad* in Modern Persian Literature Series Edited by Ehsan Yar Shater (forthcoming).

Davaran, Ardavan, *Modern English and Persian Poetry: a comparative study.* Berkeley, Ph.D. Thesis, Dec. 1973.

Emami, Karim, "Uninhibited Poetess: Forugh Farrokhzad." *Keyhan International* (July 21, 1964):6.

Farzan, Massu'd, "Forugh Farrokhzad, Modern Persian Poet." *World Literature Today,* No. 42 (1968):539-41.

Hamalian, Leo and John D. Yohannan, ed. *New Writings from the Middle East.* New York, Mentor, 1978:375-387.

Hillmann, Michael C. ed. *Major Voices in Contemporary Persian Literature, Literature East and West,* XX, Nos. 1-4, January-December 1976: "Fourteen Poems by Forugh Farrokhzad": 111-129.

———. "Sexuality in the Verse of Forugh Farrokhzad and the Structuralist View," *Edebiyat, III,* No. 2 (1978):191-211.

———. "Forugh Farrokhzad, Modern Iranian Poet." *Middle Eastern Muslim Women Speak* (Austin: University of Texas, 1977): 291-317.

Jamalpour, Bahram, abridged translations of three poems by Forugh in *Modern Islamic Literature From 1800 to the Present,* ed. James Kritzeck, Holt Rinehart & Winston, New York, 1970.

Karimi-Hakkak, Ahmad, *An Anthology of Modern Persian Poetry.* Boulder: Westview, 1978.

Klyeshtornia, V.B. "Imagery in Twentieth Century Persian Poetry." *Central Asian Review,* 13 (1965):205-215.

Lashgari, Deidre, tr. "Another Birth," "I Feel Sorry for the Garden" and "Mechanical Doll" in *The Other Voice: Twentieth Century Women's Poetry,* ed. J. Bankier. Norton, 1976.

Milani, Farzaneh. *"Farrokzad Forugh-Zaman," Encyclopaedia Iranica Online,* 2009, available at www.iranica.com.

Rahman, Munibar, "Two Contemporary Poetesses of Iran." *Bulletin of the Institute of Islamic Studies*

Islamic Studies, Nos. 2 and 3 (1964 and 1965): 64-73.

Squires, Geoffrey and Reza Nematollahi. "Contemporary Iranian Poetry." Poésie Vivante, No. 128 (1968): 3-17.

Tehranian, Majid. "Forugh Farrokhzad: The Bitter Loss." *Iranian Studies, I* (1968):53-54. Tikku, Girdhari L. "Forugh Farrokhzad: A New Direction in Persian Poetry." *Studio Islamica,* 26 (1967):149-173.

Wolpe, Sholeh. *Sin: Selected Poems of Forugh Farrokhzad.* Foreword by Alicia Ostriker. Arkansas, 2007.

Yarshater, Ehsan. "The Modern Literary Idiom." *Iran Faces the Seventies.* New York: Praeger, 1971:284-320.

CPSIA information can be obtained
at www.ICGtesting.com
Printed in the USA
BVHW072101180221
600365BV00005B/475